DYLAN THOMAS

Peter Davies

D1581283

GREENWICH EXCHANGE
LONDON

Greenwich Exchange, London

First published in Great Britain in 2005

Printed and bound by Q3 Digital/Litho, Loughborough
Tel: 01509 213456
Typesetting and layout by Albion Associates, London
Tel: 020 8852 4646
Cover design by December Publications, Belfast
Tel: 028 90286559

Cover: Photograph of Dylan Thomas © Getty Images/Hulton Archive

Greenwich Exchange Website: www.greenex.co.uk

ISBN 1-871551-78-1

to Libby

Contents

Chronology

1936	In September *Twenty-five Poems* is published by Dent. Acclaimed by Edith Sitwell in *The Sunday Times*.
1938	Marries Caitlin Macnamara on 11th July 1938. They move to Laugharne to live.
1939	Their first son, Llewelyn, born at her mother's Hampshire home on 30th January.
1939	In August, *The Map of Love*, poems and mystery stories, published.
1940	In April, *Portrait of the Artist as a Young Dog*, a collection of short stories, is published. Soon afterwards Thomas moves back to London. Finds work as a screenwriter on Ministry of Information documentaries.
1941	In Spring working on the stories of *Adventures in the Skin Trade*. His draft rejected by Dent. It will not appear until 1955. Thomas sells the four notebooks from which *18 Poems* and *Twenty-five Poems* have been quarried, thus turning his back on his early period. He writes no poetry for the next three years.
1943	Daughter, Aeronwy, born in London on 3rd March.
1944	In March the 'Little Blitz' drives Thomas and family to Sussex.
1944	In September they flee from Sussex to New Quay, Cardiganshire, to escape the V1 buzz bombs and V2 rockets. Thomas begins writing poetry again.
1945	In summer returns to London.
1946	In February *Deaths and Entrances* published to general acclaim.
1947	In April resident in Italy with his family on an Authors' Society travelling scholarship.
1947	In August returns to England, settles at South Leigh, Oxfordshire, under the patronage of Margaret Taylor, wife of the historian A.J.P. Taylor.

1949	In May moves again with his family to Laugharne, where the Boat House has been bought for him to rent by Margaret Taylor.
1949	Second son, Colm, born 24th July.
1950	February-June. Thomas's first reading tour of America – to great acclaim.
1952	January-May. Second American tour, this time accompanied by Caitlin. *In Country Sleep* published in the US in February.
1952	In November *Collected Poems 1934-1952* published.
1952	Thomas's father dies on 16th December.
1953	In March *Collected Poems* is published in the US.
1953	April-June. Third American tour. On 3rd May Thomas gives a solo performance of *Under Milk Wood* at Harvard. First performance by a cast of actors on 14th May in New York. Plans for collaborating with Stravinsky on an opera.
1953	In October Thomas embarks on fourth American tour.
1953	Dies in St Vincent's Hospital, New York on 9th November, a fortnight after his 39th birthday. His body brought home to Laugharne for burial.
1954-56	Caitlin spends much of her time in Italy.
1957	Meets the Sicilian, Giuseppe Fazio, in Rome, and settles down with him.
1963	Their son, Francesco, born.
1994	Caitlin dies in Sicily on 31st July. The following month her body is brought back to Wales and buried beside Thomas's in St Martin's new churchyard, Laugharne.

1

Death of a Celebrity

At the moment in which he died at the age of 39 in New York in November 1953, Dylan Thomas was, perhaps, the most famous poet in the English-speaking world. His death followed close on the appearance of his *Collected Poems 1934-1952* which had already in the bare 12 months since its publication, sold, in Britain and the United States, upwards of ten thousand copies – an astonishing figure for poetry at that time. It was an event that drew from the world's press, from his friends, acquaintances and even from those who had not much liked him, an extraordinary outpouring of tributes of the kind that were not, in those days before the public relations agency and its commercial agenda, normally accorded the literary man.

Over the previous twenty years, but with increasing strength from the end of the Second World War, Thomas's personality and his work had blazed a meteoric trail through the world of letters. His poetry, and the whole programme for living it seemed to represent, had caught the popular imagination in a way that, perhaps, no creative spirit had done since that of Byron. In a drab postwar ethos in which poetry was apparently happy to continue in the vein of educated introspection and self doubt that had characterized it in the 1930s, he offered something outgoing and joyous, something that appeared to banish caution and to celebrate the now.

He had also done something that neither of his older great competitors Eliot and Auden, could aspire to. He had given poetry a popularity even among non-literary people. Yet, paradoxically, he had achieved this with poems that were frequently of such perplexing obscurity that even today, meaning still waits to be teased from many of them.

This popularity owed something, of course, to the character of the 'roaring boy' he had acquired for himself in his fiery course from Wales, through the literary world of London to the bars of New York's Greenwich Village. He was the first poet of the modern age to create for himself a persona that was something akin to that of certain male protagonists of the silver screen. He had their 'star' quality, one which, alas, makes the world as interested in the disasters that attend it as in its successes.

Yet such a literary personality could not have been manufactured solely by a publicity machine or the attentions of the newspapers. In an age which was becoming increasingly dominated by radio (the possession of a set had become obligatory in this country during the war) and the gramophone record, Thomas's manifest poetic passion and belief in his creative gift was something that anyone who did not readily buy books could experience at first hand. Through those media Thomas's magnificent reading voice gave life and sense to passages of verse that might stall the reader on the page, through the sheer conviction with which he pronounced them. And his beguiling personality had become familiar even to those who might not tune into his poetry readings, through his many broadcasts (for which he always demonstrated great aptitude and professional application) on such homely and familiar topics as childhood, holidays and Christmas, always given a wry and humorously Welsh background.

All these qualities conspired to make him a legend in his lifetime. For a man with such a talent for society – especially that of a bohemian sort – this proved to be a misfortune. Many a gem-like word that might, and ought to, have been worked up into a line of poetry was poured out in bars into the ears of hangers-on who cared nothing for the poetry, but only for the reflected glory of having been alongside a slice of literary celebrity for an evening.

The words thrown out on such occasions have almost all been forgotten, except by those lucky few for whom they were not at the time totally erased by the fumes of the bottle. One gets a sense of the prodigious waste from his letters, especially those of his last years, in which the eloquence of his outpourings to friends seems to be a substitute for a creativity to which Thomas is finding it daily more difficult to gain access.

Would a Thomas of more ordered habits have produced more than he did? Possibly. But would such a man have written Thomas's

2

kind of poetry in the first place? The answer is – surely not. And we are left with the fact that, with all their acknowledged obscurities, the 89 poems by which Thomas chose to represent himself in 1952 have, in their passionate intensity and their power to illuminate dark corners, earned for him a unique position in 20th-century literature in English.

2

Cwmdonkin Drive

Dylan Marlais Thomas was born into an English-speaking family on 27th October 1914 at 5 Cwmdonkin Drive, Swansea. Though it has since been made famous by the works and doings of the poet – and through those of the American singer and songwriter Robert Zimmerman, who liked it so much he adopted it as his surname – Dylan was certainly not a common name in Wales in the teens of the last century, and requires some explanation. In the Fourth Branch of the Mabinogi it is the name given by Math, son of Mathonwy and lord of Gwynedd, to the son of the heroine Arianrhod. The tale is a charming one. Arianrhod is brought before Math who asks her if she is a virgin. She modestly replies that, to her knowledge, she is. He asks her to step over his magic wand, whereupon she is immediately delivered of a fine, golden-haired boy, to whom Math gives the name Dylan, Son of the Wave.

What brought the schoolmaster father with a baptism in mind to this particular tale can only be imagined. The second given name presents no problems. In a family which was essentially a humble one in terms of prosperity and talent, there was one undisputed luminary, a great uncle on his father's side. This was the poet William (or Gwilym) Thomas, who wrote in Welsh and took the bardic name Marlais from a small Cardiganshire river. (He actually tended to be known by another version of the name, Marles, but D.J. Thomas adhered to Marlais.) Perhaps these names, so wide of the plethora of Johns, Davids, Williams and Thomases which peopled the Welsh landscape of those days, represent a subconscious aspiration for his son to achieve what D.J. Thomas had not, and never did. He had had his own ambitions as a poet. He had aspired to newly-created chair of English at University College, Swansea, when it was established in 1920. It was not offered to him, and he remained a schoolmaster (and quite clearly a very good one) all his life. But the nickname 'the Professor', by which he was addressed locally, in pubs, shops and in the street, was a genuine acknowledgement of the affectionate respect in which his intellectual attainments were held.

D.J. Thomas's passion for English literature, which he taught, along with the language, at Swansea Grammar School, provided the mental tapestry that hung behind his son's development. He was reading Shakespeare and Milton aloud to him long before the boy even went to his first primary school. Then, at Swansea Grammar School, where he went at the age of ten, Dylan Thomas gorged himself randomly on a diet which, besides Shakespeare and Milton, included Marlowe, Blake, Keats and Henry Newbolt, and on prose writers ranging from Sir Thomas Browne, through de Quincey to D.H. Lawrence. The English Bible and the liturgy in English were also fundamental to him from an early age, both from school and in Nonconformist chapel worship. On his mother's side one uncle presided over a chapel in the Gower Peninsula, while an aunt, Theodosia, with whom Thomas often stayed, was married to the minister of the Chapel of Paraclete, in nearby Newton.

It may seem perverse to insist, at the outset, on the thorough-going Englishness of the literary diet that nurtured this, in so many ways, most Welsh of writers in English. Yet recent attempts to enlist him in the ranks of what came to be known as the Anglo-Welsh school, are not helpful. As Gwyn Jones noted when characterizing this grouping in the first edition of the *Welsh Review* in 1939: " ... the last few years have seen the emergence of a group of young writers ... who for the first time are interpreting Wales to the outside world".

This was true and remained increasingly so as Welsh writers in English sought to prove – in the face of a Welsh language renaissance which was growing in pace and strength – that they were just as patriotic, knowledgeable about, and interested in their country's heritage, and of its place in the modern world, as those of their compatriots who wrote in Welsh.

There is simply no trace of these concerns in the work of Dylan Thomas. On a basic level he was so ignorant of Welsh culture and language that he told Pamela Hansford Johnson in a letter that the given name his parent had so assiduously researched and fixed on him meant 'prince of darkness'. At the same time he told her that "it rhymes with 'Chillun', as you suggest". A man more bothered about his credentials as a true Welshman would have felt that a correct Welsh pronunciation of the name ought to have been 'Dullan'. But for Dylan, the name had been given to him simply "for some mad reason".

Thomas, both as poet and prose writer, inhabits his native Wales with total ease, and without having the slightest desire to define it or to beat a drum for it, to the English or anyone else. The bucket-and-spade Bank Holiday on a Swansea beach is to him as much a part of a nurturing culture as the remote past, and is just as glorious for the tenderness and pathos it may be witness to. The introspection – which so often sounds like regionalism – of so much Anglo-Welsh writing is at a far remove from that joyous conviction that the word 'Wales' is worth uttering because he, Dylan Thomas, is its poet.

The fact is that much of Anglo-Welsh literature is resolutely minor and does not export well. To place Dylan Thomas's name on a list containing such figures as Gwyn Jones, Vernon Watkins, Gwyn Thomas and Glyn Jones is to become immediately aware of an incongruity, of a fundamental difference in kind.

'Anglo-Welsh' Thomas may not be. Yet in another sense his Welshness is clamorously evident in his poetry, with its rhythms so suggestive of the influence of *cynghanedd,* the complex system of rhyme and alliteration of traditional Welsh verse. Yet Thomas knew no Welsh. His father, though it had been his own first language, did not attempt to teach him it. Swansea had by then become a predominantly English-speaking town under the pressure of industrial revolution and international commerce through its port. Yet the original Welsh culture stood close at its back – and still functioned in the countryside of Carmarthenshire and Cardiganshire, not so far distant. If the language was itself in retreat, its *hwyl* and *hiraeth* — passionate enthusiasm and anguished longing – were at the heart of chapel preaching, prayer and hymn singing. Through them, the downtrodden Welshman could express his sense of hope, and know himself, *sub specie aeternitatis,* as a human being.

And there was Gerard Manley Hopkins, who had in the 1870s made a thorough study of Welsh poetic method and used it to such resounding and revolutionary effect. When quizzed in later years on this influence, Thomas was apt to go quiet or sidestep the issue. In a letter of 1938 to Henry Treece, who was paying the young author of two slim volumes the tremendous compliment of writing a whole book on him, he writes: "I have read him in only the most lackadaisical way. I certainly haven't studied him, or, I regret, any other poet." As we shall see, this was disingenuous.

At Swansea Grammar Thomas made little formal progress in lessons, a severe trial to a father who was hoping for the academic distinction in his son that he had not attained himself. Yet his schooldays, and the years immediately following them, were the making of him as a creative being. Under the progressive, non-prescriptive regime of its headmaster, Trevor Owen, Thomas was able, incredibly for a school of that period, to do as much or as little as he liked. The story goes that he was detected ducking lessons by Owen and, when challenged by the headmaster, replied that he was playing truant. The benignly humorous answer came back: "Well, don't let your father [a man Owen much admired] catch you."

Thomas slacked at almost every subject except English, which he was good at, though here his contribution to classes was not of the kind that passes exams. His mental outlet was the school magazine, on which he began to shower poems almost from the moment of his getting to the grammar school.

None of these really merited preservation for posterity. Nevertheless, his school contemporary and friend, the composer Daniel Jones, reprinted a number of them in an appendix of Thomas's early work in his edition *The Poems,* which appeared in 1971 and added more than a hundred poems to Thomas's own *Collected Poems* of 1952.

Ironically, this labour of love on behalf of his old friend was inadvertently to reveal Thomas, at the very outset of his creative career, in an act of plagiarism which, since it only came to light 18 years after his death, can never be satisfactorily explained. Among the early poems in Jones's appendix was one, entitled 'His Requiem', which, in its genuine poignancy, if not in technical execution, was actually a cut above the other juvenilia, and appeared to give signs of the poet to come. It had been published not in the *Swansea Grammar School Magazine,* but appeared in what was later to style itself "the national newspaper of Wales", the Cardiff-based *Western Mail*, on 14th January 1927, when Thomas was only 12 years old.

Alas, no sooner had it been reprinted by Jones in 1971 than a sharp-eyed reader wrote in to point out that the poem was not by Dylan Thomas at all, but was the work of one Lilian Gard, a regular contributor of verse to children's magazines who had published it in *Boy's Own Paper* in 1923. Jones naturally withdrew it from subsequent editions of *The Poems*. It remains an odd episode which undeniably leaves a bad taste in the mouth. It is thankfully an uncharacteristic one, to be explained away perhaps by such an overmastering desire to kick start his career that it panicked an insecure boy into that oldest recourse of a schoolboy in a tight corner – cheating. Thomas was often a silly liar and fantasist in his life thereafter, but as far as his creativity was concerned it was not in his nature to deal in false coin. At any rate, this bruising experience of being, as it were, struck at from the other side of the grave, did not rankle with Jones. His memoir of his dealings with the poet down the years, which appeared in 1977, was generously entitled *My Friend Dylan Thomas*.

This blemish apart, at this stage of his development Thomas was, in his very imitativeness of contemporaries and predecessors, astutely practising his craft. In a Dylan Thomas poem, the effect, apparently, of a spontaneous outpouring of feeling flung down at speed onto the paper is totally misleading.

Thomas worked painstakingly for his effects. Not only that, but he had a clear idea from a remarkably early age of the kind of poet he wanted to be. As a schoolboy he was already thinking hard and discriminatingly about the poetry that was being written around him by his elders. Any idea that – whatever he may have been in his life – as a poet he was a naif, a wild man, is completely dispelled by a dispassionate article, entitled 'Modern Poetry', which he published in the school magazine when he was barely 15. It is a remarkably mature survey of a difficult period – and one still evolving – by one writing from within it.

He opens the account with an acknowledgement of the influence on the modern movement of Hopkins, against whom, paradoxically, he goes on to level criticisms of very much the same kind that were to be made of himself. "The most important element that characterizes our poetical modernity is freedom – essential and unlimited – freedom of form, of structure, of imagery and of idea. It had its roots in the obscurity of Gerard Manley Hopkins's lyrics, where, though more often than not common metres were recognized, the language was violent and estranged by the effort of compressing the already unfamiliar imagery." He is accurate on the particular strengths of T.S. Eliot, and surmises of the future: "Today is a transitional period. D.H. Lawrence, the body worshipper who fears the soul; Edmund Blunden, who has immersed himself in the English countryside; Ezra Pound, the experimental mystic, are only laying the foundations of a new art."

In the summer of 1931 Thomas left Swansea Grammar and for the next three years lived at home. There was a period of a year or so as a – spectacularly bad – reporter on the *South Wales Daily Post*. He was apt to substitute his own notion of what the world was, or what the paper's readers ought to want to read, for the unvarnished news, with often chaotic results. It was there, among the company of older men, that he realized that the pub was his natural milieu, and developed the penchant for overindulgence in alcohol that was to dominate him in a steady crescendo until the end of his short life.

Sacked from the paper after little more than a year, Thomas spent his days at home, writing verse. He also did some amateur acting at which he was actually rather good, and which stood him in good stead when he later came to direct *Under Milk Wood*. Most important, these were the three creative years from which he quarried the material for the volumes *18 Poems* of 1934 and *Twenty-Five Poems* of 1936. Swansea and its wider environs, the Gower Peninsula and the Carmarthenshire farm of his uncle and aunt, immortalized in 'Fern Hill', made him. In those years of depression the town was actually a grim place, with knots of unemployed hopelessly standing on street corners or drinking their meagre assets away in the pubs. In such circumstances political radicalism was rife, and Thomas flirted with communism himself.

But all this was lip service. Politics did not interest him. His Swansea is not one of unemployment, idle dockyards and rusting rail sidings, but its wide sweep of bay, and its beaches on which small (but important to the protagonists) human dramas are played out against a backdrop of hot summer holiday-making. In the stories which constitute *Portrait of the Artist as a Young Dog*, which encapsulates this period of Thomas's life, the effects of Depression and accompanying poverty are, perhaps, only once or twice distantly alluded to. The subject is largely that of growing up, the boy in the company of those more knowing than himself as he takes his first tentative steps in the sexual arena.

3

London: The Published Poet

Wales was the source of his inspiration, but Thomas knew that London was the only solution to his becoming published in a way that would give his work currency in the wider world. Early in May 1933, he was encouraged by Bert Trick, a much older man, an out-of-work engineer of hard left-wing views who ran a grocer's in Swansea and exerted considerable influence over the politically muddled Thomas, to send a poem 'And death shall have no dominion' to the *New English Weekly*. Its editor A.R. Orage, who had some reputation for a benign – though also muddled – socialism, accepted it, and it appeared in the issue of 18th May. (This early version was a far cry from that which was to appear three years later in *Twenty-Five Poems*.)

A 'proper' published poet, Thomas swelled with pride, shortly to be replaced by disgust when he learnt that the socialist Orage could not afford to pay for contributions. A poem he had sent to the BBC at much the same time as part of a competition, was broadcast in June, but as one of 30 accepted by the corporation for that purpose, it made no great waves.

That August, Thomas therefore set off for London himself to try and improve his fortunes, staying for some of the time with his married sister, Nancy, and her husband on their Thames houseboat at Chertsey. The visit was a qualified success. Orage agreed to take a short story from him, and Sir Richard Rees at the *Adelphi* accepted a poem. A meeting was arranged with T.S. Eliot, editor of *Criterion* and a power at Faber where his poetry list aimed to guide the destinies of the poets of a rising generation. Not perhaps surprisingly, the passionately eager, though always modest, young Welshman and the famously reserved author of *The Waste Land* did not hit it off with each other. Equally unsurprisingly, Eliot did not understand Thomas's poems. Their uncontrolled (as he saw it) enthusiasms, jarred on his academic and classical temperament and sensibilities.

Nevertheless Thomas's aggrieved perception of what he thought Eliot's patronisation of the raw young poet up from the sticks was undoubtedly misplaced. In his own way Eliot was the soul of courtesy, but it would have been expressed in an idiom with which Thomas was unfamiliar. For his part, Eliot later regretted letting Thomas slip to the aegis of his rival publisher, Dent.

Thomas returned to Swansea half deflated, but encouraged enough at the contact with London to bombard its literary editors with submissions. A batch of poems sent to Geoffrey Grigson at about that time did not find favour with the editor of the soon-to-be-influential *New Verse,* and were returned. But Thomas struck lucky in a slightly unexpected quarter, the newspaper the *Sunday Referee,* which had just announced that it was establishing a Poets' Corner, and invited contributions. Thomas had his first submission, a poem entitled 'That sanity be kept', published in Poets' Corner in September 1933. Though he could not guess it at the time, he had made the breakthrough that was to propel him to fame.

A by-product of this success was the start of his relationship with Pamela Hansford Johnson, the first serious romantic attachment of his life. It was to remain platonic – this was the 1930s, and Miss Johnson was a middle-class girl. Thomas, in whom a strong puritanical streak always lurked, was inexperienced enough at 19 still to tolerate such an arrangement. Besides which, he probably had an instinct that a contact such as her, with an 'in' with the London literary establishment, might be no bad thing to cultivate. And his correspondence with her (preserved on her side but not on his) gave him a London penfriend with whom he could trade literary theories and ventilate creative aspirations on gloomy Swansea winter evenings. She was later to make a reputation as a novelist with *This Bed Thy Centre,* and, ultimately, become the wife of C.P. Snow. But for the time being she was a poet, and a fellow contributor to Poets' Corner.

Poets' Corner, which was run by a psychologically fragile but sweet-natured bisexual called Victor Neuberg, did more than publish individual poems. It undertook a Poets' Corner book prize, which entailed the *Sunday Referee's* sponsorship of a volume of poems.

Thomas's congratulations when the first of these prizes went to Hansford Johnson, and not himself, are given somewhat through gritted teeth in his correspondence, and followed close at heels with an offer to help her to edit her early poems (which he evidently thinks are shockingly bad). When the volume appeared, in November 1933, he allowed her to be "capable of achieving perfection in a certain type of poetry, a poetry born out of Christina Rossetti and the Georgian and Poetry Bookshop Gang". She does not appear to have resented his remarks – which were actually not far wide of the mark.

In any event, he was soon to follow her. On 25th March 1934, the *Sunday Referee* announced that Dylan Thomas had won the second of its Poets' Corner prizes. Shortly afterwards Geoffrey Grigson accepted two poems for his *New Verse*. At about that time, too, his poem 'Light breaks where no sun shines' was published in the *Listener*, the literary periodical of the BBC. It caught T.S. Eliot's attention, and he began to feel he might have been hasty about Thomas's work. Thomas began to feel like a man honoured, at least among peers.

But for the moment, of greater éclat than this appreciation was the public's reaction to the opening lines of the second stanza: "A candle in the thighs/Warms youth and seed ..." Whatever subsequent reviewers might complain of Thomas's obscurity, the readership of the BBC's august organ were quite clear that the corporation had published an obscene poem, and letters of complaint reached the BBC by the sackfull. Sir John Reith, the austere director general of the BBC, was a man of the purest Calvinist principles. The corporation's senior staff were appalled by the *Listener*'s lapse. It was widely credited in and outside the BBC that a six-month ban had been issued against the publication of material by Dylan Thomas. Whether true or not, it did him no harm. To Thomas, to be notorious was a far better state of affairs than being merely respected.

Having awarded its prize to Thomas, the *Sunday Referee* now found itself in some difficulty over the finances of publishing his volume, and a period of indecision ensued. Thoroughly disconsolate after the first flush of the award, Thomas offered the poems to Eliot at Faber, who had written to him after his *Listener* debut. But when faced with the stark choice Eliot was indecisive too. In the end a partner was found in the David Archer bookshop, an idealistic left-wing establishment in Parton Street in Holborn. Nine months after the prize had been awarded *18 Poems* appeared under the *Sunday Referee* & Parton Bookshop imprint in December 1934.

The reviews were slow in coming. The *Sunday Referee* stood by their man as a matter of course. But it was not until the new year that other journals and papers began to notice the newcomer. But as the *Listener, Spectator, New Verse* and *Times Literary Supplement* all gradually added their voices to a chorus of acknowledgement, if by no means unanimous praise, over the next few months, Thomas might well consider himself satisfied. The verdict of *Time and Tide* that the volume was "the sort of bomb that bursts not more than once every three years", was music to his ears. Even the sullied columns of the *Listener* found a reviewer to concede that "this is one of the most remarkable volumes of poetry to have appeared in the last few years" – and that in spite of the fact that *18 Poems* included the offending 'Light breaks ...'

The pool of poems on which Thomas drew for *18 Poems* was actually the same as that which provided the raw material for *Twenty-Five Poems*, published two years later. In that sense, the volumes might be assessed together, since many of the poems in the latter were actually begun before some of those in *18 Poems*. On the other hand, Thomas not only went constantly to his stock to revise and rewrite, but he put a lot of thought into deciding the form of each volume and the impact it would make. As a debut offering *18 Poems* offered the reader certain themes which Thomas wanted to introduce as his preoccupations at that time – and is entitled, even at this distance, to a separate assessment on that score.

(It is interesting that Daniel Jones's 1971 edition, *Dylan Thomas: The Poems*, which takes the poems out of the volumes in which they were published, arranging them as nearly as Jones can determine, chronologically in order of composition – with the addition of much previously unpublished material – gives a far less satisfactory, much more diffuse, result than the *Collected Poems* of 1952, which adheres to Thomas's own arrangement.)

There is no getting away from the fact that these early poems are difficult. Thomas attained to a greater simplicity as he went on. The injunction of Hopkins to Bridges: "Take breath and read it with the ears, as I always wish to be read, and my verse comes all right", does not always work with Thomas, but it carries the reader a long way. Thomas was a bard, and envisaged his poems being declaimed. What strikes one immediately in this supposedly 'prentice work is the confidence of utterance, the ease of identification of the poet's self with what is of fundamental importance in the created world – quite apart from the immense technical assurance. Early in the volume we come across one of his most famous poems: "The force that through the green fuse drives the flower/Drives my green age ..." It is a poem which confronts the reader simultaneously with the strengths and difficulties of Thomas's image-making procedures. Its opening line is one of tremendous power. Not surprisingly it has been attempted as a visual image by a number of artists. The suggestion is of irresistible procreative force, gametes colliding in fusion to produce the zygote and a new generation of being. The word "fuse", though ostensibly here a noun, takes on the life of a verb, to suggest an almost rainforest impetuosity of reproduction. The very next line confronts us with the decay to which this generative force is rapidly propelling us. The poet, in the centre of this process, is "green" with youth, as the growing plants are. But the juxtaposition of this epithet with "age" foreshadows, at the same time, his decline and death – and that of the physical universe whose burden he here shoulders.

In the last stanza Thomas seems to be hinting that time, which in the rest of the poem is hell-bent on our destruction, may nevertheless have reserved a heaven for us in the stars. He is: "dumb to tell a weather's wind/How time has ticked a heaven round the stars." Why is one is reminded irresistibly of Juliet's ecstatic: " ... cut him out in little stars/And he shall make the face of heaven so fine/That all the world shall be in love with night."? But if it was Thomas's intention to hint at some sort of redemption here, he appears unwilling to sustain it. An earlier version, published in the *Sunday Referee* the previous year, had the relatively lame line "that time is all", instead of "How time has ticked a heaven round the stars". It would have been more consistent with the poem's overall meaning, but for some reason Thomas moved away from it. It may be an example of Thomas's image-making running away with him, and leading him into fields of meaning that he had not thought through. At any rate, at the end, the poem returns decisively to its opening suggestion of death within life. The poet is: "dumb to tell the lover's tomb/How at my sheet goes the same crooked worm." Again, though there is no direct allusion to the scene, Romeo and Juliet, both alive, but shortly to be dead and decaying in their vault at the end of Shakespeare's play, come indelibly to mind. Thomas's poems have the power to suggest to us, without in any sense plagiarizing, the themes of other poets.

With all its obscurities 'The force that through the green fuse ...' is an immensely rewarding poem if persevered with. It remains an astonishingly assured performance from a man not yet twenty. It is not difficult to imagine its impact on the poetry-reading public of the 1930s.

It is a truism that sex is a fundamental component of Thomas's poetry. And in some ways it is. Yet in his poems (in marked contrast with his prose) he never really attempts to handle sex as part of a personal relationship – in short, as part of love. In the later poems, notably and magnificently in 'In the White Giant's thigh' it is powerfully evoked as the life force that is fundamental to the continuation of the universe. In *18 Poems,* sex is almost always an unfulfilled, thwarted business.

'I see the boys of summer' was the poem with which Thomas chose to open the volume. It is in essence a dialogue between age and youth – though the poet (himself 'a boy of summer') is the conduit through which the viewpoint is established and the theme felt. In this poem of three movements, the *senex* voice has the first word: "I see the boys of summer in their ruin/Lay the gold tithings barren". As far as age is concerned, the prognostications for youth are gloomy ones. But this is not just a rhetorical device as a framework for debate. The doubts are deeply felt by the poet himself.

The boys of summer are no sooner glimpsed than they are seen "in their ruin". The very action of their being renders the "gold tithings" barren. Thomas's use of this ancient word, signifying small communities and their land holdings in the Saxon system of frankpledge, has the effect of linking his lament with those of Old English poetry. These boys, like the grasshopper of Aesop, have no care for harvest.

So far the theme has not been overtly that of sex. Then "their girls" are introduced. But there is to be no springtime of love here. Love is frozen even before it ripens. The imagery is somewhat imprecise, but the meaning is clear enough. The boys can get no delight from the opposite sex. The apples, which (besides the hint of sexual activity implied by the fruit's role in the Fall) may stand as storehouses of knowledge and memory, will never ripen for them, but be drowned before summer is out.

In the last stanza of the *senex* movement, this mood of disillusionment deepens as the movement closes with its central, sexual, preoccupation: "I see that from these boys shall men of nothing/ Stature by seedy shifting". The very ejaculation of semen will be a "seedy shifting", as the adolescent, unable to express his sexual desires in relationships which will be consummated, masturbates instead.

To this, in the poem's second movement, *iuvenis* can at best reply: "In spring we cross our foreheads with the holly,/Heigh ho the blood and the berry". The tone of the stanza's opening lines, with its desperate, deliberately facile echoes of the jollity of wassail (at the same time darkened with hints of the crucifixion), cannot be sustained. We are soon returned to the poem's central theme, the (for the adolescent) futility of the whole sexual project. "Here love's damp muscle dries and dies". Love's "muscle" is undoubtedly, here, not damp with female secretions as it pleasurably subsides from tumescence after a bout of lovemaking. We are unmistakably with Mr Bloom on the beach in James Joyce's *Ulysses,* gloomily enjoying solitary relief after his Nausicaa, Gerty MacDowell, has done her best to expose herself to him: "Mr Bloom with careful hand recomposed his wet shirt. O Lord, that little limping devil."

'I see the boys of summer' may not be totally consistent in its imagery. It undoubtedly contains excrescences and oddities which are not digested. But the overall aim is clear. In an age (Joyce, Lawrence and a few other pioneers apart) long before today's sexual explicitness, it attempts honestly to explore that baffling paradox: the adolescent male's possession of rampant sexual desire, before he can usefully 'do anything with it'. It also expresses that sense a still-young male has (probably no less relevant today) of not quite achieving a sense of usefulness or sense of direction in a world run by adults.

'If I were tickled by the rub of love' moves us on to an unmistakable engagement with the idea of sexual relationship and its consequences. It is a powerful poem, yet one pervaded by a sense of distaste – amounting almost to resentment – at the thought of sex, and what it imposes on male freedom: "If I were tickled by the rub of love,/A rooking girl who stole me for her side,/Broke through her straws, breaking my bandaged string". Here, "rub" acquires two meanings. On a basic level it is the frotting of sexual congress. In another sense it is the rub of Hamlet's "ay there's the rub". It thereby gives a weighty dimension to the responsibilities (in terms of pregnancy/children) inherent in the sexual act, at the same time imparting to "tickled" a sense of entrapment (as the trout), even while it retains its simple meaning of the excitement, both physical and mental, of sexual activity. And it is not a piece of naked misogyny breaking in, that the female in the contract must be "a rooking girl", robbing the man of the sexual initiative?

The sense of the rest of the stanza is clear enough, and perhaps one should not try to unpick the images. The implication of the next line is that the predatory girl has burst out of her straws/stays/(?), and compelled the man to deploy his previously "bandaged" member for procreative purposes.

Thomas then goes on to say that (in spite of this predatory raid on his sexuality) he would not fear the consequences of the apple (the biblical fall) nor the biblical flood: i.e. sin and its destruction on a global scale. Yet the tone of the stanza rather belies this. Spring, in which this copulation would presumably take place, is for the poet a season of "bad blood" from which no good can come.

The next stanza continues the idea that the play, so to speak, has been taken away from the man. The issue has been decided by forces beyond his control: "Shall it be male or female? say the cells,/And drop the plum like fire from the flesh." The refrain, "I would not fear ...", which recurs throughout the poem, is at odds, here, with the manifest refusal to take pleasure in the fact of a birth. Instead, the newcomer becomes an inanimate fruit, which nevertheless somehow sears a fiery way out of the bearing mother's body. Rather like the child in William Blake's poem 'Infant sorrow' this infant has entered the world only at the cost of its mother's agony. Yet, as in Blake's poem, it seems to have done so almost as an already sentient being – or even something more. "Winging bone" sprouting in the heels carries a suggestion of Mercury, the gods' messenger, bursting from the womb to bring, however, no comforting assurances.

Discomfort is the theme here, as Thomas ingeniously fuses images that suggest simultaneously – and with deliberate unpleasantness – the pleasure of sex and the pains of birth. The flesh of the copulating male is tickled by the pubic hair through which the baby will also "hatch" on its way into the world. The baby's thigh, innocent though it is of any sexual intent at that point, is nevertheless the product of man's "itch", and somehow cannot escape that taint. The implication is that the infant, too, will go on to face the sexual dilemmas of its procreator.

Of course, this is seen from the standpoint of a young man not long out of adolescence who, later in the poem, is encountered contemplating "rehearsing heat upon a raw-edged nerve" (again masturbating). As the poem proceeds, Thomas piles image on disgusted image: "Time and the crabs and the sweethearting crib/ Would leave me cold as butter for the flies". Decay, disease and death are the natural corollary of sexual activity. The mother, cooing over her baby in its cradle, is brutally juxtaposed to the crablice which infest its father's pubic hair (presumably as a result of his traffic with women of the streets). And the author of this act of procreation is left as a rancid pat of butter, flyblown on a dish, as the scummy waters of an advancing tide obliterate everything. In the remaining stanzas we are not returned to the refrain of "I would not fear … " The poet's neurotic loathing has carried him impossibly far beyond it. The sexual dystopia he creates is so vividly realized that the poem's closing lines can hardly be expected to sustain whatever conviction is implied by them. Thomas has done his work of painting the fearsome consequences of the sexual act too well to allow either himself or us repose in so trite an assurance.

There is a temptation to place 'Especially when the October wind' in the line of declamatory birthday poems that includes the later and much better-known 'Poem in October' and 'Poem on his birthday'. It is an October poem, the month of Thomas's birth. But whereas they look back, from the standpoint of a man now, in T.S. Eliot's phrase, "in the middle way", 'Especially when …' is by a man at the beginning of his poetic journey. The poet, conscious of his bardic calling, sets out his stall.

It is a far cry from the neurotically-charged atmosphere of the foregoing poems. The poet is in an almost serene mood as he surveys his demesne and soaks up the detail of the landscape he knows and loves so well: its wild ravens croaking out over the sea shore and, as he turns his mental gaze inland towards the town of Swansea, its women gossiping in knots and children playing in the park. October, the month of his birth, is a fitting time for the young bard to open to us some of the themes he will be sharing with us in his passage through experience. In a pleasant conceit in which he dons the guise of the medieval Maker, he promises to unlock the speech of trees and water to us: "Some let me make you of the vowelled beeches,/ Some of the oaken voices …". In the next stanza, the "pot of ferns" and the "wagging clock", return us to the mundanities of the human world we shall meet later, when Thomas plays bard in an even more imperious mood to his dead aunt, "dead, humped Ann", in 'After the Funeral'. But for the moment it is the natural world in which the poet invites us to take this walk, communing, as he does, with nature: "Some let me tell you of the raven's sins." Like some Jerome in the wilderness, he is so intimate with the ravens that inhabit it, that he is familiar with the wrongs they have committed. Above all, in the last stanza, the "loud hill of Wales" – on one level, the hilly backdrop to Swansea Bay, on another the hills of the whole land, and on a third its eloquent people – will be induced to commune with us, courtesy of the poet's powers. On the few occasions Thomas utters the word "Wales" in his poetry, he manages to make it pregnant with meaning.

There is, of course, a dark element to be faced up to, and that is the creative effort the poet must make, on our behalf, to enable him to give voice to these secrets. At the end of the first stanza the busy heart shudders with the effort, as she "Sheds the syllabic blood" that articulates her perceptions. At the end of the poem we are warned, again, that "the coming fury", i.e. of themes darker and more troubled than that of this poem, will, too, exact its toll, draining the poet's creative heart.

Finally, to "Light breaks where no sun shines", which, since its incendiary debut in the *Listener,* has been, along with "The force that through the green fuse drives the flower", among the most quoted of Thomas's early poems.

The opening stanza is a good illustration of John Ackerman's assertion that: "Thomas's early poetry contains many instances of profound and striking images surrounded by an incomprehensible density of language." The antithesis of the first line is such an arresting one, appears to be on the verge of revealing so much, that we almost *want* it to be worked out within the poem. And we are prepared to stay with it as far as "the waters of the heart/Push in their tides", which seems to be going somewhere. But the whole thing collapses into absurdity with the entry of broken ghosts and glow-worms.

Thomas has effectively to kick-start the poem again in the second frame, with: "A candle in the thighs ..." The introduction of a sexual theme seems to take us in a different direction, dispelling the moody reflectiveness of the opening. But this is not sustained. We cannot follow the "fruit of man" to its apotheosis in the stars. ("wrinkled" and "fig" might have been a good metaphor for the scrotum, but whatever idea was in Thomas's head, he has failed to control it.) And the last line, which might, or might not imply, that the "candle in the thighs" has, in the upshot, somehow failed to fulfill its potential ("no wax" – no semen?), brings the train of thought to earth again.

There is no need to labour the point. Yet, although at this distance many of these early poems have a dysfunctional feel about them, they still have a power to guide the senses. It is not difficult to see the source of their impact on the literary world of 1934. They offered a full-blooded neo-Romantic assault on the academic classicism for which poets like Eliot and Auden, C. Day Lewis and Stephen Spender stood, and maintained their position at the heart of the English poetic Establishment. This gale-force blast from the Welsh fringe seemed to take poetry out of the study. It restored it, if not exactly to "the flowery lap of earth" – as Mathew Arnold described Wordsworth's impact on the world of 'correct' 18th-century poetic sensibility – then certainly to a place where "birth, copulation and death", in the words of T.S. Eliot's Sweeney, ceased to be the topic of glib drawing-room chatter, and were to be savoured in their primal agony and stench.

4

Caitlin Macnamara

The period between *18 Poems* at the end of 1934 and the publication of *Twenty-Five Poems* in September 1936 transformed Thomas's life. London was responsible for much, though not all, of this development. After several visits from Swansea in 1934, Thomas moved there in November that year. In a remarkably short time the shy provincial boy, living with his mother and father at home, had become the thorough-going bohemian, a seasoned habitué of the pubs of Fitzrovia and Soho. At the Fitzroy Tavern, the Marquis of Granby, the Wheatsheaf, the Swiss and the 'French', impecunious writers hung out, drowning their poverty in drinks, bummed from hangers-on of all shades. This louche comradeship of indigency, frequently descending into drink-fuelled rancour and spite, persisted in Soho until comparatively recently, until, that is, poets ceased really to be poor any more.

It suited Thomas, who was a compulsively companionable man. But it was also the beginning of that threat to his creativity which lay in his being such a marvellous verbal entertainer on his feet – provided the drinks were coming, and there was an audience to listen to him. At such a time any man was Thomas's friend, who could provide the liquid wherewithal to furnish yet another bout of dazzling improvisation. And this might continue until the performance, over-fuelled by alcohol, lapsed into tiresomeness and incoherence.

Of course many writers, when they are, as it were, 'stood down' from the serious business of creativity, do not want to be reminded of the hard task that awaits them on the morrow, and the morrow after that – and on every day for the rest of their lives, as long as they are able to hold a pen. Flippancy, clowning, or in some cases, a self-awarded licence to be merely morose, are a safety valve. On the other hand, the side Thomas showed to these boon companions who, as it were, put their money in the slot machine and purchased themselves a groatsworth of wit, could be irritating in the extreme to old friends. Those who had made a journey, and kept the rendezvous, especially to chew the fat with a man they had, perhaps, not seen for some time, would be repelled by these displays of self-centredness, staged for complete strangers.

In his perceptive study, *Dylan Thomas: The Biography*, Paul Ferris recounts a recollection of Gwen Watkins, wife of another long-suffering, but true friend of Thomas, the poet Vernon Watkins. In a crowded public house, where Thomas had, as usual, been 'performing', she halted him in mid-flight for a moment by doubting that he was at bottom a serious man. Clearly genuinely hurt by the charge, he turned and began to give her his full attention, while he explained that poetry such as his could be written only by a fundamentally serious person. For a moment she thought she might be on the verge of access to the 'real' Thomas ... and then, as she recalled, "a hanger-on touched his shoulder, and 'instant Dylan' was turned on again".

London was important to him, for allowing him in those early days before he became famous himself, to rub shoulders with the likes of Geoffrey Grigson, William Empson, Norman Cameron, Rayner Heppenstall, whose practical influence and help was important to him. He might, to them, bemoan the provinciality of his native Wales, but it remained creatively vital to him. In London, he was like a sailor released on an extended run ashore after a long spell at sea. Nights ending in oblivion followed by heavy-headed mornings, awoken to on the floor of one acquaintance or another – or, later, in the bed of one woman or another – before the drinking began all over again, were the enemies of writing. To do that he had to make frequent retreats to Swansea and later, Laugharne. In between, came temporary berths in Cornwall, Ireland, Dorset, Cardiganshire, Gloucestershire, Oxford, wherever some sort of patronage could be found, to regroup and remind himself who – and why – he was.

He learnt to be something of a womanizer, though, as it seemed to his friends, often more for public consumption than private satisfaction. The vein of Welsh puritanism ran deep. Unlicensed sexual activity was the more piquant if it could be sin. He, on occasions surprised both male friends and women companions by the vehemency of his reaction to a couple embracing hotly and careless of censure, in a bar or on the street.

His relationship with Pamela had survived the confession he made to her in his now famous letter from Wales of May 1934. "Oh darling, … I've wasted some of my tremendous love for you on a lank red-mouthed girl with a reputation like hell."

This shook Miss Johnson, as well it might. Elsewhere in what is a suspiciously well-crafted letter, Thomas spares her none of the details. It may be that the whole episode is fictional, designed to emphasize to her the danger that other women present to a man of his attractions, and to bring their own relationship to a head. (It goes without saying that the so-freely calumniated partner in this, necessarily drunken, encounter, has, in his male conceit, to have fallen in love with him.)

At any rate Pamela 'took him back' after this lapse. But her object was marriage, and though he did thereafter propose that to her, she remained sceptical. "Comrade bottle" as she put it, always seemed a higher priority to him than she was. Over the succeeding months ardour gradually subsided into a kind of mateyness. Well before the end of the following year they had ceased to love, and gone their separate ways.

At what point his drinking became a life-threatening affair, is difficult to determine. The "DTs" described in his letter to Pamela is clearly an exaggeration. The man was still only 19 and had only been drinking beer. Had he stuck to his favourite bottled mild, or the small ales that were on tap in the pubs of west Wales in those pre-strong lager days, one imagines no great harm would have come to him. In photographs, the winsome cherub of 1934 becomes merely the somewhat portly cherub of 1945. The gross figure standing with a tumbler of spirits at the bar of the White Horse Inn on Hudson Street, in New York's Greenwich Village in the early 1950s is a very different matter. Even in the poor quality of the available photographs he looks like a man whose life is on the skids.

But in the mid-1930s all that was many unhappy years in the future. In the spring of 1936 he met Caitlin Macnamara. He had always said to friends, even women friends, that his idea of a woman life-companion was something "dumb and lovely". Caitlin was not dumb but she was lovely and, the considerable vicissitudes of their life together apart, she was to irradiate his being like no other woman. The daughter of an Irish father and a half-French, half-Irish mother, whose marriage had broken up, she had had an unconventional upbringing. She had been a chorus girl "at the London Palladium" – but, in reality, probably at far less exalted venues. She had gone to Paris, but could find no work there. In London where Thomas met her, she sometimes displayed her uninhibited Isadora Duncan-derived movements at parties after a few drinks. In Hampshire, where she moved after her divorce, her mother had been a neighbour of Augustus John, for whom Caitlin modelled. Having been routinely seduced – or perfunctorily raped – as most of his models were, she was, when Dylan Thomas met her, the famous artist's mistress.

Her portrait by Augustus John, which hangs in the National Museum of Wales in Cardiff, shows her as a woman of tempestuous beauty. A mane of corn-gold hair, a nose almost, but not quite aquiline, and a neck that is strong rather than fine, all contribute to a sense of restless energy barely contained within her frame. She was powerful and athletic from her dancing, and swimming, which she loved. At the same time she was actually shorter than Thomas – which pleased a man conscious that, at little over 5ft 6in he was of under-average stature. Yet in photographs she looks the more substantial of the two. There is always something soft-focused, tending to podginess, about his outline. Nothing could be more incongruous than the famous picture of them taken in 1938, in which she snuggles up with dutiful submissiveness against his chest. She looks full of a latent power, ready to uncoil and strike, at the first sign of an external threat to this young lovers' bliss.

Their first momentous collision in London (the canonical story is that, after being introduced by Augustus John in the Wheatsheaf, they went off together and spent several nights at the Eiffel Tower Hotel, putting the experience, unknown to John, on his bill) was a beginning, not a resolution. Both had other relationships to work through. But Thomas knew he wanted to marry her, and eventually went to Cornwall in pursuit of her. There, after he had finally extricated her from John, who nevertheless continued, to Thomas's annoyance, to hang about her, on 11th July 1937, they were married in Penzance register office. The 'honeymoon' was in Mousehole.

A man whose life was in almost every other respect barely under his own control, Thomas made, in this instance, an extraordinarily right choice. To say that their marriage thereafter was one of 'ups and downs', in the conventional phrase, is putting it mildly. They drank too much together with the inevitable results. They fought like cat and dog, she generally the assailant, going at him with fists, bottles or kitchen utensils. They were serially unfaithful to each other, he rather because it was par for the course at the end of a boozy evening apart from her in London to fall into bed with a star-struck admirer. Her adventures stemmed from a delight in the exercise of a genuinely uninhibited sexuality. She was conscious of her lithe dancer's body and its power over men. She loved to flirt. Why should he have all the fun that was going in that department?

And yet he had made a marriage which preserved his health and sanity for far longer than they might otherwise have survived. She created a home and sanctuary for him, where he could lick – and she could tend – his wounds, whenever he crawled back from London. On less than little money, she brought up his three children, cooked his meals, and improvised, in many temporary homes but finally, in the Boat House at Laugharne, the oasis of peace in which he could compose his poems. A vivid writer herself, as her later books demonstrate, she nevertheless cared about his creativity and fought – not always at the right moment perhaps – against those whom she saw as predators on it. He, in his turn, doted and depended utterly on her. Perhaps only one of his other dalliances – a product of one of his American tours – ever came anywhere near threatening that. But by that time his life was in free fall, and he had gone well beyond being aware of what was good for him and what was not.

5

Twenty-Five Poems

Twenty-Five Poems was published on 10th September 1936. This time there needed to be no Heath-Robinson coalition of the kind that had attended the birth of *18 Poems*. Richard Church, at Dent, the publisher of the remarkable Everyman series, had from the year before, indicated his interest in anything further that Dylan might produce. At heart a deeply conventional man, he seems to have hoped against hope that Thomas would somehow 'grow out of' his early manner – and was alarmed to find that he had not. Quarried from the same notebooks that had given rise to *18 Poems*, this new batch of work took him aback with its unrelenting obscurity, and in the violence of its imagery.

He havered, annoying Thomas on the way by describing him as a surrealist. (The London Surrealist Exhibition of summer 1936, at which Thomas read a poem, somewhat belatedly brought this European movement to the notice of the British public.) It was a charge Thomas forthrightly rebutted. He pointed out that however incoherent his poems might be, that could only be the fault of technical failure on his part. His poems were about flesh-and-blood life, and were meant to be understood concretely, and not "through the pores", as he put it, like the dreams and fantasies of surrealism. In this, unlike his disclaiming the influence of Gerard Manley Hopkins, Thomas was being honestly self-aware. To address himself to an intellectual movement such as surrealism claimed to be and acquaint himself with its theories was simply not in his nature. His work was to come from within himself or not at all.

Somewhere within *himself* Church recognized that he had a poet of quality on his hands, and took his life in his hands. *Twenty-Five Poems* came out to a mixed reception. Those who had, as it were, gone out on a limb for *18 Poems*, realizing that they were taking a punt into the unknown, felt slightly cheated. If they had hoped to see from the second volume, where the first might be leading, they were disappointed. *Twenty-Five Poems* seemed, in most respects, to show no development, no advance on its predecessor.

But one opinion did matter, that of the grande dame of English letters at that time, Edith Sitwell. And her notice appeared not in a literary periodical, but in *The Sunday Times*, whose reviews were highly influential in forming the opinions of the middle classes in cultural matters. From disliking Thomas's work at the outset, she had come round to him, and her verdict: "I could not name one poet of this, the youngest generation, who shows so great a promise ... " had a miraculous effect on sales. *18 Poems* had been bound in an edition of 250, many of which had not been sold. The first printing of 750 copies of *Twenty-Five Poems* sold out almost immediately. Further impressions were called for and within little more than two years 3,000 copies had been sold. This was a figure which put him on a par with Auden, perhaps the best-selling serious poet at that time, and one certainly much more easy to understand. As – if not more – important to Thomas than the sales, was the imprimatur of such a grand figure as Sitwell. That moment dates the beginning of his fame.

Yet Grigson and the doubters were, perhaps not really wrong in their cavilling assessment. Leafing through the volume we find little that is as immediately arresting as was, in its predecessor, for example, 'The force that through the green fuse drives the flower'. The impression is overridingly that of 'more of the same' – rather to be expected from poems drawn from the same stock as the previous volume. And since the surprise value (to try and imagine it from the standpoint of contemporary critics) has gone, that disappointed many of the critics.

In his book *Druid of the Broken Body*, Aneirin Talfan Davies has been the most loyal advocate of Thomas's qualities as a poet. He bases his assessment on a conviction that Thomas is a religious poet, and that the poems of this volume demonstrate a "remarkable insight into the sacramental nature of the universe". He is certainly not wrong to be struck by what seems to be an instinctive recourse to the language of religion. What other poet of that age of scepticism, frequently verging on cynicism, could give poems such titles as 'This bread I break' and 'And death shall have no dominion' – and mean them?

The volume's opening poem, 'I, in my intricate image' sees Thomas again as the bard/Maker, at the centre of the physical and mental universe – which is where he likes to be. I do not propose to analyze the whole poem. It is a long one, in three movements and, does, I think, collapse under the weight of diffuse imagery and unconnected propositions. The first stanza gives the flavour: "I, in my intricate image, stride on two levels,/Forged in man's minerals, the brassy orator". By the time we have negotiated the first three lines, the meaning is already becoming difficult not merely to follow, but even to sense. Thomas, is, it would appear, stating a duality in the poet's nature, but he does not stop to address the conflicts implied in this, as a 17th century poet, having opened the theme, would have gone on to do. He is, apparently, 'normal' man, forged from the same elements as his fellows. At the same time, as "the brassy orator/ Laying my ghost in metal", he takes on the mantle of the bard, one of Shelley's "unacknowledged legislators of the world".

Later in the poem the poet's notion of the intricate image appears to have acquired other dimensions. His "images stalk the trees and the slant sap's tunnel". As some kind of woodland spirit, he now walks in the heart of nature, at one with its humblest inhabitants, insects and nettles. But there is no real sense of progression. By the end the powerful promise of the opening lines has been windily dissipated in a poem that is too long, and too diffuse.

A somewhat simpler proposition (apparently) is the apparently sacramental 'This bread I break'. Both Aneirin Talfan Davies and John Ackerman see in this poem evidence of the poet's sense, as Ackerman puts it: "of the sacramental nature of the universe: the common things of life serve to illustrate profound mysteries, which are themselves witness to, and celebrate, the Creator". But is that actually what is being asserted here? It seems to me that Thomas either means something quite different, something much more disillusioned, and is using the terms of the Eucharist to emphasise that, or that, in the process of building meaning from individual words – which was his admitted practice rather than to search for words to express meaning – he has lost control of his material.

The tone of the opening stanza: "This bread I break was once the oat,/This wine upon a foreign tree" is very unlike the terms of the Eucharistic liturgy – which does not, after all, concern itself with the origin of either bread or wine. But Thomas, significantly, does, and in doing so seems to come to the conclusion that in the process of being crushed into wine, the grape's "joy" – in being a happy grape on its vine bush – has become broken. And there is an ambiguity introduced, in that the grape's present state of unhappiness might not have come about through man's meditated actions, but rather through the random violence of the wind. Yet this notion is not made germane to what one takes to be the theme of the poem. It remains merely a distraction – a distraction such a short poem can hardly afford.

In the next stanza it is the oat's turn to be considered as being in a state of pristine merriness, before Man came on the scene: "The oat was merry in the wind". Man is again a destructive predator, breaking the sun, pulling the wind down. The wind, with which the oat enjoyed a happy symbiosis while it nodded, hanging from its stem, has now been robbed of its power to give that simple pleasure.

The final stanza does nothing to dispel an overall tone of sourness that is quite unlike the reconciliation with God that is implicit in the Eucharist. The poet now occupies a situation analogous to that of the oat and grape of the first stanzas. His body and blood are identified with the bread and wine of the Communion. But one searches in vain for any sense that the poet/grape/oat are thereby unified in a victory over sin and death, which is what the Eucharist represents. We, the reader, are, on the contrary, apparently charged with letting the grape/wine/blood "make desolation in the vein". Some taint has been introduced into what would normally have been a state of spiritual exaltation. The final line, far from carrying us into the "peace that passeth all understanding" has a decidedly tetchy quality about it. Something has gone wrong with the sacrament, and that something, is our/Man's fault. "My wine you drink, my bread you snap" suggests a breaking of French sticks and a gulping them down with wine at a picnic. The whole synthesis of the sacrament seems to have been deliberately turned on its head.

Now Thomas may often become muddled in expressing precise meaning, through the sheer size of the arsenal of the words at his disposal, and his sometimes reckless method of deploying them. But his tone seldom fails to be an accurate reflection of the sense. And the tone here is certainly not that "God's in his Heaven and all's right with the world."

The celebrated 'And Death shall have no dominion' is a very different matter: Dead men naked they shall be one/With the man in the wind and the west moon". Thomas stays constant to his opening proposition, which is simply – as advertised – "death shall have no dominion". We would search in vain here for any other underlying meaning, and the thing is as simple as the church blessing.

After complaining about Thomas's frequent obscurities, it might seem almost churlish to object, here, to the almost complete lack of metaphorical density. It is certainly uncharacteristic of Thomas at that date. The image of the drowned man achieving an apotheosis in the heavens, once his bones (and presumably his spirit) have been picked clean is evocative in a charming sort of way. But its charm is that of a painting by Murillo, and hovers perilously close to the borders of sentimentality. A more serious objection, it seems to me, is that Thomas is not a parson but a poet. Priests hand on truth, but we expect poets to work for it. The apparent serenity of the refrain seems not to have been truly striven for within the poem, with the result that the assurances of the conclusion, as Yeats would have put it, "lack all conviction".

Thomas never dabbled in politics. He almost never even alludes to the tremendous events in the outside world. The six years (a long time in a life so short as his) of a war that, apart from anything else, devastated his native city, are alluded to in only a handful of his poems. And they are certainly not 'war' poems, but the use of the primary consequence of war – death – to reflect on the condition of being human. Or, in the case of the death of infants, of the implications for the rest of us of not having been allowed even to become human. 'The hand that signed the paper' is overtly political. Its subject appears to be the destructive nature of bureaucratic tyranny in our times. "Five sovereign fingers taxed the breath,/Doubled the globe of dead and halved a country" suggests the turbulent 1930s: Hitler's annexations; Mussolini's East African carve-up; the cynical fascist overthrow of a democratically elected Republican government in Spain. But the date on the manuscript, now in the Lockwood

31

Memorial Library at Buffalo, New York State, is August 1933, by which date Hitler had been in power little more than six months, and none of the other tremendous events on the trail to world war had yet shown themselves. Perhaps Thomas was thinking subconsciously of the Versailles treaties of 1919, which had dismembered Austria-Hungary and taken large chunks of territory from the Kaiser's Germany. His recourse is, anyway, to see contemporary events in biblical terms: "The hand that signed the treaty bred a fever,/And famine grew, and locusts came". The poem has been much praised. (Partly, one suspects, as a reflex of sheer relief – it can be readily understood.) Even the otherwise largely inimical Martin Seymour-Smith allows it to be a "small success". But, as so often with these early Thomas poems, succeeding stanzas do not show any development of the opening proposition. The final one seems to state the sublimely obvious. The inertness of "Hands have no tears to flow" is one of those examples (which we have noted before but which are, thankfully, rare) of Thomas having somehow 'given up' on image-making and, seemingly, just wanting to get out of the poem while the going is good. In his account of the poem, in his – far from uncritical but nevertheless sympathetic – essay of 1957, G.S. Fraser, doing his best to find some virtue in *Twenty-Five Poems*, sorrowfully stigmatizes it as "an example of bathos".

'I have longed to move away' is a much more personal poem than any of the foregoing. The bard of 'In my intricate image' and the priest of 'And death shall have no dominion' have taken a back seat here. The voice of the man, as poet, or simply as man in his society, is paramount in: "I have longed to move away/From the hissing of the spent lie". It is possible to take the poem in several ways (or to read it on several simultaneous levels). It can be taken as a turning away from the outmoded and now, for the poet, no longer effective formulae of traditional religion; it might be that the poet is discussing himself as a man growing up in, and rebelling against, the social mores of his times. (The tone is certainly Prufrockian to a degree almost never felt in Thomas elsewhere.) Or this may be a discussion of creativity itself, of the poet seeing himself in relation to other poets (and their success), and considering what might be the price of altering course in an attempt to enjoy a degree of that. The poem might, of course, contain elements of some, or all, of these three considerations.

Ackerman is in no doubt that this is essentially a poem about the difficulty for Thomas of religious belief, that it is a "picture of Thomas as a lost Nonconformist, wrestling with an inherited religion and a Puritan ethos ..." But the poem is actually almost completely free of religious imagery. One has to clutch at straws to see a reference to the Fall in the "hissing of the spent lie", or a distaste for the monotonous forms of worship in "repetition of salutes".

Ackerman here insists on a Thomas "wrestling between religious doubt and an imagination haunted by biblical myth and language". But Thomas, in general, never gives any sense that there is a conflict between his religious upbringing and his creative being. Indeed, the latter joyfully feeds on the former with increasing thankfulness as the poetic œuvre unfolds. The imagery and the liturgy of worship are the bricks and mortar with which Thomas enthusiastically builds his poetic castles in the air. Far from being a source of conflict within him, something with which he must either come to terms or conquer, they are a poetic sine qua non.

There is certainly no sense in this poem that religion is the source of his disquiet, whatever else it is that he fears to become enslaved by. By the same token, it seems to me that Thomas here is not, either, giving vent to a conventional gripe about 'society', as such images as "spent lie", "half convention" and "half lie" might be enlisted to demonstrate. Neither in his poems nor in his short stories does he ever 'put down' his background, his family nor the humble people among whom he grew up. Whatever criticisms of these might escape him in his letters, there is, in Dylan Thomas the poet, very little of the satirist. This, too, sets him apart from most of the writers of the 'Anglo-Welsh' school, whose very insistence on their Welshness demands that they are able, at the same time, to have a maturely critical attitude to it.

It seems to me that what does deeply concern Thomas in this poem is the threat to his creativity that might come from himself, if he is weak enough to harken to "the hissing of the spent lie" – that is, the exhausted vein of poetic preoccupations he finds in the work of so many contemporary practitioners. Oxford, Cambridge and Harvard, with their highly-developed social consciousness and sophisticated cynicism, rule the roost, and in the second part of the poem Thomas is " … afraid;/Some life, yet unspent, might explode/ Out of the old lie …" Is Thomas here saying that he actually fears that his own poetic impulses might be corrupted by the pervasive influence of this school of pseudo-sophisticates, or does he merely mean that he fears that he might become disheartened by the fact that being of that school appears to be the only route to recognition as a poet, and that he might have to capitulate to it? If so, he dismisses that possibility. He will not succumb to "night's ancient fear", which seems roughly analogous to the "old terrors' continual cry" of the earlier part of the poem – i.e. simply childish fears of inadequacy and failure. Nor shall "pursed lips at the receiver" – perhaps the "hissing of the spent lie", now being insinuated down the telephone in an attempt to undermine his resolve, succeed in derailing his creativity from its chosen track. If die he must – here, creatively rather than literally (though for a 'total' poet like Thomas creative death might as well be accompanied by bodily extinction) – it will not be by some "half convention and half lie". The repetition of the word "lie", in one context or another through the poem, underlines the poet's anxiety about the frailty of poetic truth in an age when a good deal of cynicism and falsehood, as he sees it, is being published by the magazine editors and routinely hailed by the reviewers.

As we have seen, the poems of both *18 Poems* and *Twenty-Five Poems* were selected by Thomas from the mass of work he had already completed before the first volume was published in 1934. The exception is 'Altarwise by owl-light', a sequence of ten sonnets, and the most ambitious project in *Twenty-Five Poems*. Its composition began in 1935, after the publication of *18 Poems*, and continued over the next year. It clearly marks for Thomas an important stage in his development, and was placed at the end of the book. (As such, it is probably the only poem in either book, whose position in its volume reflects its place in an order of composition.)

It was the poem selected by Edith Sitwell in her influential *Sunday Times* review to carry the burden of her praise. Her verdict was: "nothing short of magnificent in spite of the difficulty".

To critics – generally the Welsh ones – who have tackled the poem, it marks a decisive engagement with religion for Thomas. Certainly it is shot through with religious imagery. Its very form seems to invite comparison with the great sonnet sequences of the

17th century. That said, the "difficulty" conceded by Sitwell, persists.

All critics are, I think, agreed on the extreme difficulty of 'Altarwise by owl-light'. I agree, and I think the demonstration of these difficulties at length would be a futile exercise. This, from Sonnet V, is characteristic: " And from the windy West came two-gunned Gabriel,/From Jesu's sleeve trumped up the king of spots". Biblical imagery runs riot here, as never before in Thomas. But we find ourselves asking: to what purpose? The opening conceit – the archangel Gabriel arriving on the scene as a gun-toting card sharper – is a striking one to which it is difficult not to want to respond. But the atmosphere of the bar, of card-playing, of drinking, is not made to work by Thomas to make intelligible whatever is intended by his "Byzantine Adam" falling down "on Ishmael's plain". Thomas does not seem to be able to make real for us his intended equivalent between western saloon and his own assumption of the mantle of Adam.

Sonnet VIII, with its crucifixion theme, promises the greatest seriousness of the ten. It is a piece of scene painting whose vivid power recalls, almost, the Crucifixion of Grunewald which forms part of the celebrated Isenheim altarpiece at Colmar. Crushed by grief, the mother of Christ is "Bent like three trees" – seeming to bear the weight of the entire three crucifixes and their cargoes. Through her shift we see her breasts pathetically shrivelled – "bird-papped" – almost to nothing. Wrung dry by sobbing, she can weep, not now the great water drops which alone would do justice to her immense sorrow, but only tears like "pins". Meanwhile the poet as Christ – and at the same time a witnessing bystander? – is drabbled with the blood still pumping from his own guttering heart. Christ's wound is also the world's, and the world's tribulations. There seems also a sense in which Thomas (in a flight a little too far-fetched) seems to say that it is also connected with 'Eve's wound' – "the long wound's woman" – through which Mary has borne Jesus, and is therefore in some sense the author of this scene.

The sense of Christ on the Cross as being Everyman raises its head again in a strikingly irreverent image: "This was the sky, Jack Christ, each minstrel angle/Drove in the heaven-driven of the nails". "Jack Christ" may simply be seen as a 'Jack the Lad', one of us, though the Jack in the Green, the unquenchable Green Man of

Arthurian legend, who on having his head struck off, simply picks it up and rides away, is also suggested. "Each minstrel angle" (Pope Gregory's "Not Angles but angels" seem to have crept in here, in a typical Thomas failure to leave an image alone, but take it one step further into obscurity, or, as here, plain silliness) seems now a willing participant in a process which will, on the third day ("three-coloured rainbow" – three sunsets, three dawns) see the miracle of the salvation leaping "From pole to pole").

I grant the poem is not as completely effective as this reading (which has dwelt on its strengths) has made it sound. The "snail-waked world" is a bathetic image for – if that is what Thomas intends – a world only slowly awakening to forgiveness and glory. "Unsex the skeleton" carries too much of an echo of Lady Macbeth's frightening invocation to the powers of evil to be an effective component of a poem which is moving towards the conclusion "Suffer the heaven's children through my heartbeat". This takes us back from the terrific events of the crucifixion and their aftermath to the calm ministry and quiet wisdom of the Christ of St Mark 10, 13-16.

Thomas's meaning is not in doubt. Lapses of taste apart ('taste' perhaps not the appropriate word – in Thomas one thinks rather of an excessive deployment of imagery, which obscures his sense of what is appropriate) this eighth sonnet uses the New Testament story, to unfold a vision of reconciliation that is genuinely felt. Thomas has moved away from a mere shifting around of biblical furniture to create an effect.

The question of its merits apart, 'Altarwise by owl-light' marks a decisive step in Thomas's technical development. After it, he leaves the wilfully obscure rhetoric of the 1933-34 poems behind him. (Such of them as continued to form the basis for later published work are reworked out of all recognition.) As Daniel Jones puts it: "In comparison with the almost claustrophobic denseness of 'Altarwise by owl-light', the later poems create an effect of release and, as it were, 'ventilation'."

6

War

For a number of years after their marriage the life of Dylan Thomas and Caitlin was to be a peripatetic affair, largely dependent on the mercy of friends. (His family briefly put them up from time to time, but it was in her mother's Hampshire home that their first child, Llewelyn, was born in January 1939.) Thomas had first been to Laugharne with his friend the writer Glyn Jones in 1934. In 1938 the author Richard Hughes (of *A High Wind in Jamaica* fame, and now fresh from the laurels of *In Hazard*), who lived there, found him and Caitlin a fisherman's cottage that was to provide them with a home of sorts for the next two years until the need to find work drove him back to London in the war years. It was not until 1949 that the patronage of Margaret Taylor, wife of the historian A.J.P. Taylor, led to the Boat House that became the bolt-hole of his last years (and has since become a place of pilgrimage).

In the meantime Laugharne suited Thomas. Its small scale, its readily accessed society, a decent pub, (the famous Brown's Hotel) were all congenial to him, giving him the stability he needed, combined with the opportunity to pop out for a sustaining tipple without falling into that sycophantic company which was his ruin when he went to London or further afield.

The Welsh are not in awe of a poet, and they took him as he was. Not unlike the modern Greeks (before that culture was violently assailed by the baneful apparatus of commercial holiday-making) they took him as a poet in his society. There, he was a craftsman among other craftsmen – farriers, choirmasters, hedgelayers, singers, essayists, the makers of crabpots and fishing nets – as Welshmen expect any man of letters to be. They saw no need to lionize him as an exotic figure. He reciprocated by talking among them as man to man. Supping his small ale in the bar of Brown's Hotel, he was under no pressure to deliver those later performances for public consumption that were to be the waste of so much of his creative intensity.

At home, meanwhile, Caitlin, pregnant with their first child, kept house. Among her fortes was the production of a succession of those gross-sounding stews which nevertheless soaked up the lunchtime alcohol and propelled him to the room where he did his writing in the afternoons. It was a brief, happy time, such as neither of them would ever know again.

And then came the war. It was disastrous for Thomas. Now it may seem preposterous, to be granting a totally disproportionate importance to the concerns of literature, even to trifle with the idea that the life and work of a single poet could weigh as anything against a conflict that killed tens of millions, reduced millions or more to utter misery and was witness to some of the vilest acts that have defaced human history. Of course it cannot. And yet, as one thinks on Thomas as the events of 1939 unfold, one cannot help feeling sorry for him.

Thomas cut a wretched figure. For one thing he was a completely apolitical animal. Even his attempts at dodging the call-up lacked any conviction. He completely fluffed playing the 'pacifism' card. How he did eventually manage it is still not quite clear, though it seems 'asthma' came to his rescue at one medical.

The fact was that neither he nor his poetry had, to that point, concerned itself with human life on the level of social justice or moral right. The human being for him might stand under God or heaven, but to face a future clouded by the violent doings of tyrants was something for which his being was utterly unprepared. The glib authority of 'The hand that signed the paper ... ' was to be cruelly exposed.

Thomas would find, of course, that he was not mentally alone. In the pubs of London where poets and other sorts of writer gathered to see what they might salvage in terms of making a living, he would meet plenty of kindred spirits who wanted to avoid the war, without being able to persuade themselves that they were genuine objectors on grounds of conscience. But war had come at completely the wrong time for him.

He was little more than beginning on his poetic course, both in terms of the development of his inspiration and of his publishing career. And now, the sources of that inspiration, the waters, bays, hills and fishing villages of West Glamorgan and neighbouring Carmarthen, were to take on a very different hue. It was very difficult to pierce through the hellish pall that now enveloped them – the barbed wire, tank traps, pill boxes, coastal artillery, and above all the racket of anti-aircraft guns and the bombers that came by night – and still envisage, as he wanted to, the heron, the cormorant, the seal, in the holiness of their being, and a people going about their innocent ways under a Welsh heaven.

Thomas's was a nature not to be able to have a valid attitude to the experience which now seized the rest of the world – not even that which Yeats had adopted 'On being asked for a war poem' in the previous conflict: "I think it better that in times like these/A poet's mouth be silent ..." Nor, if the spirit did eventually react to the war, was there to be any 'Welsh airman foreseeing his death' for Thomas. He did not have Yeats's sense of history. He was probably more genuinely steeped in his community than Yeats was. But he lacked the kind of analytical education that would have enabled him to consider the individual psyche, place it in its social and historical context, and give it a plausible and moving reason to confront blind forces of destiny, as Yeats did in 'An Irish Airman Foresees his death'.

And then, his publishing career, too, had only just got under way in 1939. After the puzzlement that greeted his second volume he desperately needed to consolidate and extend his reputation. As it happened he was at a point of new development with the project that was to follow *18 Poems* and *Twenty-Five Poems,* and give impetus to it in both verse and prose.

The Map of Love, a mixture of poems and short stories, appeared on 24th August 1939, just 10 days before England declared war on Germany. Hardly surprisingly there were not many able to spare the time to give it ear.

Reviews were mixed. The erudite and influential Cyril Connolly conspicuously took against it in a review in the *New Statesman*, in which he complained: "The technique remains, the inspiration gone." He, too, was to change his mind after he had founded his periodical *Horizon*. More important to a Thomas who was impecunious and likely to become more so if such a verdict carried any weight, was the almost total commercial failure of the venture. Of the 3,000 copies of the sheets printed by Dent, fewer than 300 had been sold by the end of the year. Many of the sheets remained unbound.

It has to be admitted, even at this distance, that such a *mélange* as *The Map of Love* was not calculated to show off Thomas's qualities. It was certainly not the ideal sort of launch platform for the poet who wanted to be seen as having 'moved on'.

The volume consisted of 16 new poems and seven short stories. Now the latter are not the realistic stories of childhood and adolescence that have since become known – if for nothing else, for their sub-Joycean title – as *Portrait of the Artist as a Young Dog*. They are a mixed bag in an earlier vein of fantasy that invited a reawakening of the charge of surrealism. In fact, the stories of *The Map of Love* owe far more to Poe's *Tales of Mystery and Imagination* than they do to surrealism. There is nothing of dreamland, and the subconscious in them. They have both charm and the power to disturb in equal measure, but they are essentially the work of a hyper-imaginative child.

Characteristic of them is 'After the Fair', which may well be the first story Thomas ever wrote. It was first published in *The Criterion* in 1934. In it, a strange young girl steps out of the shadows in the aftermath of a busy day of commercial activity at the fairground and proceeds to exert what seem to be magical powers on the fair's Fat Man. In a completely different vein is 'The Tree', also written in 1934. It is one of a series of stories embedded in a strange and fictional location over whose inhabitants the presence of religion always hangs, with generally baneful consequences: "There was an idiot to the east of the country who walked the land like a beggar." The very cadences of the prose are biblical, and Thomas goes on, in an atmosphere of mounting sinisterness, to relate how the idiot is drawn into a re-enactment of the crucifixion by a strange child who inhabits the valley.

These stories have made their reappearance from their re-publication in *A Prospect of the Sea* (1955) onwards. They read like the work of a precocious teenager. They were strange stuff to publish in harness with the poems of a man by then in his mid-twenties and wanting to show that he had safely negotiated the attentions of what Connolly has, in a memorable title, called 'The Enemies of Promise'.

The notion of 'simplicity' when applied to a poem by Dylan

Thomas, is a relative one. Nevertheless we detect in some of the poems of *The Map of Love* (though even here, some refer back to that intense production of 1933-34) an intention, at least, to provide us with narrative clarity. These are, by and large, much more personal poems. Though by that one does not mean poems enclosed by specific relationships. Thomas does not write, for example, about identifiable women – as lovers – except in a couple of cases where he does seem to be making atonement to Caitlin ('I make this in a warring absence', 'Not from this anger'). Rather, he now seems to become capable of recreating for us the experience of someone else's life, without, as in the early poems, trying to place himself – and his adolescent sexuality – in the centre of it. On a most fundamental level he has, of course, grown up. Marriage and parenthood have, simply, taken him out of himself.

'The tombstone told' is an example of this new simplicity. Contemplating the grave of "A virgin married at rest." Thomas projects himself imaginatively into the ghastliness of the wedding night as it was for so many innocent girls of that era: "Before she lay on a stranger's bed …/She cried her white-dressed limbs were bare". Thomas has got beyond the self-obsessed resentment of sex – and of woman's part in, and demand for, it – that was so ineluctably a component of the early poems, and found a new compassion.

'The tombstone told' is a beginning on a road to greater lucidity and broader sympathies. (It is one off which Thomas frequently falls, right to the end of his creative life. There are still, in *The Map of Love,* poems which revert to the clotted images of the early manner.)

In 'Especially when the October wind' Thomas had set out a bardic manifesto in his refrain: "Some let me make you of … " in which he promised to speak to us of "all I know", through his discourse with trees, water, meadows, autumnal spells and "the loud hill of Wales". It may seem to the reader to have been a long wait for this vow to be discharged. But it is triumphantly done in 'After the funeral', a poem which soars far above anything else in *The Map of Love* and is, in my opinion, among the finest half-dozen poems Thomas wrote. Its subtitle is 'In memory of Ann Jones'. Its first 20 lines unfold its matter in a single, magnificent sentence.

The Ann Jones of the title is, of course, his aunt Annie, on his mother's side, who had married Jack Jones, the slovenly tenant of the Fern Hill farm near Llangain in Carmarthenshire. There Thomas had spent the sort of childhood days that are never forgotten and become an imperishable part of one's being. She had died of cancer in 1933, five years before this version of the poem was completed. But her death is only the starting point for Thomas, now. She has ceased to be merely his affectionately-remembered Aunt Annie, who once valiantly dug out her carefully-hoarded tinned peaches and proudly set them before the wealthy mother of a friend of her nephew's who came to stay – only to have the magnificent gesture spurned (an incident recounted in the short story 'The Peaches').

Whatever Thomas's reaction to her death at that time, it is no longer important. (An apparently callous reference to the "cancered aunt on her unsanitary farm" in a letter of that year to his friend Trevor Hughes may, I think, be set down as a species of cynicism an adolescent in any age might use to disguise real hurt. Interestingly, a callow early attempt at this poem, done hard on the heels of her death indicates how far he was from coming to terms with it.)

This recollection of her in 1939 is to be scarcely short of apotheosis. Yet the development of the opening lines is a muted one. It in no sense prepares us for the trumpet blasts to come. It begins with random exterior details, dealt with in a tone of mild contempt: the indifferent mules, with their flapping ears (though their mournful brays seem, comically, to want to voice a requiem on their own account); a blind man's peg leg (he, too, is close to death, and associated at the same time with the closed eyes of the corpse and the lowered drapes of the funeral parlour); the rheumy eyes of mourners; their salt-encrusted sleeves (possibly the effects of weeping eyes crushed into them, or simply of sweat exuded by garments that badly need laundering); the sound of the sexton's spade; the apparent (completely random and incidental?) suicide of a derelict youth (who also stands for the desolate boy Thomas); the mourners both tearful and prickly with each other; and then, the familiar stuffed fox and the potted fern of the typical Welsh 'front room'.

But Thomas has no intention of staying with the fashionably down-beat here. There could scarcely be a greater contrast with Auden's, roughly contemporaneous, 'In Memory of W.B. Yeats, d. Jan 1939', with its carefully distanced 'scientific' refrain: "What instruments we have agree/The day of his death was a dark, cold day." In Thomas's elegy the parochial detail with which he has been trifling with us is swept imperiously aside. The shrivelled woman who has just been consigned to earth is transfigured as a titanic being. Her life-blood, her great-hearted 'holy' kindness, stand as the life-giving element that enriches the parched humanity of Wales. She may have required in her humility "no druid of her broken body", but Thomas has elected himself her champion. In an image which is the very embodiment of *hwyl*: " ... I, Ann's bard on a raised hearth call all/The seas to service that her wood-tongued virtue/Babble like a bellbuoy ..." the druid, in the possession, now, of those miraculous powers with which he once undertook to interpret the speech of the waters to us, shakes his Neptune's trident. The metaphor is a severely compressed one, but it suggests irresistibly that the obedient sea will rock and ring every bellbuoy, whose clangour will then articulate virtues the expression of which has hitherto been locked up in her wooden tongue.

The 'holiness' engendered by the broadcasting of Ann's spirit has nothing to do with religion. Here, religion, personified by the mourners who have proved inadequate to perceive the holiness of what they are mourning, has completely failed. Far from needing the Church's conventional assurance of eternal life, Ann's virtues, imbued now with a power that seems to have nature at its beck, will. "Bow down the walls of the ferned and foxy woods/That her love sing and swing through a brown chapel". Ann has become almost a pantheistic deity, flowing through the very veins of the natural world. And we are reminded, in the homage she compels from "the ferned and foxy woods", of the acute contrast between her new domain and its vital denizens, and their lifeless counterparts, the shrivelled and stuffed witnesses of the uncomprehending obsequies indoors.

We are returned to the fern and the fox in the closing lines of the poem, which Thomas concludes with a magnificent rhetorical flourish. We had previously seen Ann transformed by the suffering that had her "face died clenched on a round pain" into a statue in the poet's mind. Now it is as a serene image that he will always remember her, when he recalls her uncomplaining virtue, suffering and holy kindness. As her bard-elect, he is under a double injunction not to betray his vision of her. In the final lines he exhorts her marble hands and his own 'hewn' poet's art, never to allow him a moment's quiet in the endless contemplation of her life.

Only in that passionate degree of remembrance and affirmation, will "The stuffed lung of the fox" ever be able to "twitch and cry Love/And the strutting fern lay seeds on the black sill".

7

Portrait of the Artist

It is, I think, a pity that Thomas's next collection of short stories, which was published in April 1940, had to be given the title *Portrait of the Artist as a Young Dog*. It seems, for perpetuity, to pigeonhole the production as being, in essence, second-string Joyce, which it is not. Thomas's collection of stories may not have in it things of such magnitude as Joyce's *Portrait of the Artist as a Young Man*, but it is in no sense trying to ape Joyce. Thomas was a man of very different sensibility, and his metaphysical bent, if we may so describe it, expressed itself, too, very differently. The moody, self-analytical, always intensely intellectual introspection of the Irishman, playing over the rigours – and terrors – of a Jesuit education, on its way to achieving creative self-expression, is as unlike the tender simplicities of Thomas's work as possibly could be.

Then, again, the title *Portrait of the Artist as a Young Dog*, even if we do not allow it to turn us towards Joyce, but take it on its own merits, expresses something completely at odds with what we actually encounter in this collection. Far from being an account of the adventures of some precocious *vert galant*, Thomas's book takes him from a childhood which is largely rural in feeling, through an adolescence which is the very reverse of a passage through the fleshpots, to a young manhood which is still capable of wondering puppy love.

But there we are. Thomas is on record as saying to his friend Vernon Watkins that the title was a flippant one, but that he had chosen it because it was likely to have commercial appeal. Evidently Dent felt the same. And so we are stuck with it.

These stories turn their back decisively on the genre represented by those of *The Map of Love*. There is no mystery – apart that is from the innate mystery of Welsh eccentricity and foible. These are realistic stories which retail the doings, observed often with the gentlest of mockery, of ordinary beings. The best are those which use Thomas's early experience for fictional purposes, rather than merely recording events, and extracting the quaintness from them, on the way. Thus 'The Peaches' in which Aunt Annie's proffer of tinned fruit is spurned by her grand guests is, though full of charm and observation, a little too much of a stereotyped homage to the honest virtues of the Welsh lower middle class. And Uncle Jim, Annie's slovenly and generally drunk husband, Jack Jones, is a little too much a Welsh stereotype as he sits in "his special chair which was the broken throne of a bankrupt bard".

From 'The Fight' the fourth story of the collection, we are out of childhood and into young pre-puberty, and from this moment sexual curiosity and awareness gains on the young protagonists. Strangely, in these stories, Thomas seems to have none of the deep-seated problems he encounters with sex in his poems. The 'naughty' high spirits of the classroom down the ages, are captured with effortless economy.

In 'Extraordinary Little Cough' we have moved on a couple of years. The school friends are old enough to spend time away from home on their own, in this instance "to camp for a fortnight in Rhossilli, in a field above the sweeping five-mile beach". Thomas captures the heart's ease of young spirits, as they ride on top of the lorry that carries them and their camping gear towards their destination. And then the run down through the fields towards the cliff top. Suddenly, the atmosphere of innocent anticipation is marred by a return of the disagreeably familiar. As they near the edge of the cliff: "... two broad boys were wrestling outside a tent. I saw one bite the other in the leg, they both struck expertly and savagely at the face ... They were Brazell and Skully." We keenly share in the boys' utter mortification. What was to have been a carefree holiday is ruined in an instant. And to add to their humiliation enter – girls:

"Rather to our surprise as onlookers, one of 'our' party, Sidney, who seems to be the oldest and boldest of them, happens to know one of the girls, and makes introductions. The urgent optimism of puberty is immediately at work. Brazell and Scully are forgotten. The upshot is that the narrator finds himself walking on the cliff alone with the object of his heart's desire: "Brazell and Skully were two bullies in a nightmare; I forgot them when Jean and I walked up the cliff ..." Alas for him, Jean hasn't. As he enthuses passionately to her, imagination clumsily outrunning truth in his desire to please, he is brought down to earth, when she says: "Who was that handsome boy on the beach, the tall one with dirty trousers?" The game is up. Brazell and Skully have not been wasting their time. And now, when they all meet up again, Brazell moves in, instinctively knowing in this situation 'what a girl wants' – which, in the case of a relatively simple organism like Jean, is certainly not the babbled enthusiasms of the narrator. The day ends in ruination. Uncomplicated animal attraction (aided by the greater age and experience of Brazell) triumphs effortlessly over the romantic desires of the younger boy.

By 'One Warm Saturday' which brings the volume to a close, the Dylan Thomas protagonist is a young man. On a day of high summer he has declined an invitation to go to Porthcawl's Coney Beach, "where his friends were rocking with girls on the Giant Racer, or tearing in the Ghost Train down the skeletons' tunnel". In a half-melancholic mood he strolls the sands of Swansea Bay, now half-heartedly joining in a game of beach cricket, now pausing to listen to the "hell-fire preacher" lecturing to a congregation of indifferent women.

This is the nearest we come, in this collection, to a mood of Joycean introspection. A man, and a poet, contemplating wasted hours that should be devoted to creativity, he is nevertheless able to sneer at his attitude of assumed superiority to these mundane activities, wishes perhaps that he had accepted the invitation of "Herbert, in his low, red sports car, GB at the back, a sea-blown nymph on the radiator". He walks on into a municipal park, Victoria Gardens, with its seaside flower clock: " 'And what should a prig do now?' he said aloud, causing a young woman on a bench opposite the white-tiled urinal to smile and put her book down." The fact that she is reading a book, rather than sitting watching the boys go by, imparts to our view of her the suggestion that she may be of a thoughtful cast, which makes her an object of greater interest – to us and him. The white-tiled urinal opposite which she sits is an immediately ambiguous detail in a man so little given to the kitchen-sink as Thomas is. Perhaps it has a bearing on what later transpires.

In the meantime, he looks, lingers, and is lost in love. Though he is now of an age when imaginings of intimacy with a girl go well beyond a hand-holding and a hug on the beach, the protagonist remains, here, essentially the tongue-tied boy whom we saw on Rhosilli cliffs. Though the "girl in a million" accepts the homage of his gaze, he cannot respond and hurries shamefacedly on.

He flees to a deserted pub where the barman's random garrulity jars on him, while it uncannily strikes to the heart of his sense of failure. The dialogue here could have been written by any one of a dozen English writers from the 1940s to the 1960s. One can certainly imagine it occupying a corner of a Kingsley Amis novel. The difference is that for Amis it would be merely a bridge passage of that bar chat at which Amis excels. In the hands of Thomas, here, it becomes an exquisitely-judged counterpoint to his protagonist's self-flagellation.

Yet for the protagonist all is not lost. As he sits supping his beer in morose solitude, the vision from Victoria Gardens suddenly enters the pub, accompanied by two other women. From their badinage with the barman, it is instantly evident that none of them is the refined innocent of Thomas's fervent imaginings.

Suddenly recognizing him as the shy and shamefaced boy of the afternoon, she invites him to join her and her friends. More drink is taken and in the increasingly approximate atmosphere, she is soon allowing his advances. His grand infatuation effortlessly survives the knowledge, shortly introduced, that she is, in fact, waiting for the middle-aged fancy man who finances her life. And the arrival of this lover, at some point in the evening, fails to dampen his optimistic assurance that the evening is to end in love's fulfilment for him.

There is a magnificent absurdity in the magnitude of the protagonist's self-delusion, which Thomas handles with compassionate humour. Perhaps the girl really does like him. She seems a good-hearted soul with a reservoir of love for more than one – but someone has to pay her bills. They all go back to a party in her room at the top of a lodging house. There, still in thrall to his conviction that he is somehow going to make away with Lou under her fancy-man's nose, he misses his way to the lavatory, to which he has been directed by the lover. Too drunk to find his way back to the room, after blundering about in the darkness he gives up, descends to the ground floor, and finds himself alone outside in the night air.

I have dwelt at some length on what is, after all, a collection of only 10 stories which occupy little more than a 100 paperback pages, because it seems to me that they contain Thomas's best – in the sense of truest – work in prose. Granted that they are so strongly autobiographical, Thomas is always able to preserve a distance between himself as author and a protagonist who is, effectively, himself. This is a remarkable achievement, which enables him to continually keep his central character under an objective scrutiny.

These stories emphatically give the lie to the notion that the 'real' Thomas is the uncaring, rip-roaring, womanizing drunk of public myth. Indeed, he did not begin writing them until his mid-twenties, by which time he had decidedly embarked upon that side of his career. In them, he achieves, it seems to me, a dimension of insight, a degree of interest in human beings, that was completely absent from the 'magical' stories of *The Map of Love,* and has become something else by *Under Milk Wood* – something showier, more theatrical. There is, in these stories, absolutely nothing 'knowing' about Thomas as narrator.

Here, on the road from childhood to manhood, he holds various scraps of humanity in his hands, and plays upon them a gaze of compassionate tenderness. Above all, he never betrays the innocence of the heart's imagination.

Adventures in the Skin Trade

Adventures in the Skin Trade was not published until 1955, two years after Thomas's death. It was mainly written in the spring of 1941, i.e. after the stories of *The Portrait.* It was evidently intended to carry the story of the growth of the artist's sensibility amid the scenes of his native Wales, on to its development in the London that was his next port of call. It remains a fragment, and at that a rather unsatisfactory one. The symbolic acts of vandalism its protagonist commits in his parents' house in the small hours before leaving it to catch the early train to London are overdone, and somehow compromise the integrity of the thing before it really gets off the ground.

Thomas seems uncertain of the framework within which he is operating. There are dreamlike sequences interspersed with the familiar realities of pub and bar. The scene in which he finds himself drunk and naked in a bath with the naked Polly, who seems willing to seduce him, is perhaps the most successful in embodying the impact of the moral vacuum of Bohemian London life on the boy up from the country. But – his generally drunken behaviour with women apart – Thomas's nature actually tended to abhor the moral vacuum. In *The Portrait* he could make us like the pub women of Swansea, with all the dishonesty and superficiality of their desires, because he could show them to have, at the same time, kind hearts and to be totally devoid of malice.

The apparent seediness of London is another matter. He does not understand what has created these women and makes them behave in the way they do. As a result he is not able to make come alive for us any redeeming qualities that might lie at the heart of this milieu.

Thomas sent the first 10,000 words of *Adventures in the Skin Trade* to Dent. If they thought they were going to be receiving the great autobiographical work of fiction they anticipated, they were to be bitterly disappointed. Indeed, they disliked it intensely, and said as much. Readers' reports were along the lines of: "at best it is a fragment of frolicsome dirt", and "running amuck, with emphasis on muck". More ominous from the point of Thomas's future, not only with Dent but with any publisher, was the perception that as a writer, he was going backwards; " ... unless he pulls himself together he is going to fizzle out as an author most ignominiously".

Vernon Watkins was staying with Thomas in Laugharne when Dent's letter arrived. Whether any of the severer reflections of their readers had found their way into it, is doubtful. But it made its point. They would be returning the manuscript, hoping to see "something different" (i.e. something much better) at a later date. Thomas was utterly deflated. True, he had no great belief in the book as a piece of art to be judged by the side of his poems. But he was convinced that he had at least produced something commercially attractive. For a poet like him to have stepped down from the lofty slopes of his high calling, to produce something lesser, but supposedly at least life-saving, only to be found wanting in this inferior genre, was not merely galling, but a deep humiliation.

8

Creative Crisis – And Recovery

In the spring of 1941 Thomas sold the four notebooks from which the entire contents of *18 Poems* and *Twenty-Five Poems* had sprung, to a rare book dealer. From this dealer they made their way to America and today reside in the Lockwood Memorial Library of the University of Buffalo, New York. For Thomas it was a calculating farewell to the intense creativity of the Cwmdonkin Drive period. At that stage he seems to have been in a highly cynical frame of mind. He certainly cannot have known whether the muse would ever step in and take his hand again.

On an evening during the early stages of the London Blitz, Thomas had been introduced to Donald Taylor of Strand Films, a company which was making documentaries for the Ministry of Information. Thomas had, from childhood, been a passionate enthusiast for the cinema, though without any notion that he would want to write for it. The two men hit it off. Taylor hired Thomas, at first in sound production and then, realizing that Thomas's enthusiasm for the medium readily translated into an aptitude, as a screenwriter. A salary of £20 a week, a good deal in those days, was to keep him afloat for the rest of the war. Work for the Ministry of Information also absolved him from any fears that a sudden reclassification of his physical state might render him liable to call-up. During the period he was involved with it, Thomas was to devote himself to this work with surprising conscientiousness and self-discipline.

None of this cut any ice with Caitlin. She had fallen in love with a poet, not a film studio hack. As far as she was concerned Thomas was selling his soul to the devil, and Taylor was his Mephistopheles. On the evidence who can gainsay her? Thomas had only produced a dozen poems in the first two years of the war. Now, from August

1941, he was not to write anything as a poet for almost the next three years.

Quite apart from his being diminished in her eyes by his film work, for Caitlin the compensations of this new financial competence were not apparent. Little of Thomas's handsome salary ever seemed to find its way into her purse. While Thomas was in London her shiftless existence continued, sometimes with him, sometimes not. She was constantly on the move. She and her infant son Llewelyn, lived with Thomas's parents in the tiny house at Bishopston that had succeeded 5 Cwmdonkin Drive. Then, when Swansea was bombed, she removed to a small cottage at Talsarn, near Lampeter, in Cardiganshire. In between there were visits with her mother in Hampshire, where Llewelyn spent a good deal of the war.

For a period from the autumn of 1942 there was a more settled existence in Chelsea, where Thomas rented a studio, and their daughter Aeronwy was born. Then came the Little Blitz of spring 1944 and a move to Bosham in Sussex, whose atmosphere of armed preparation for the impending invasion of Europe Thomas hated. By autumn the assault of the V1 flying bombs and V2 rockets was under way, necessitating a move back to Wales, this time to New Quay in Cardiganshire.

This makeshift existence – and seemingly chronic accompanying penury – bleeds seamlessly over into the post-war period. From the moment he leaves New Quay and returns with his family to London in September 1945 there is a stream of frantic pleas from Thomas to friends and acquaintances, canvassing a cottage in Hampshire or a flat in Chelsea. There is a sojourn in Beaconsfield with Donald Taylor and two periods in Oxfordshire, courtesy of Margaret Taylor, wife of the historian A.J.P. Taylor, (who, for whatever motives – and they do not seem to have been sexual – was considerably kinder to Thomas than she was to her own marriage, which eventually collapsed under the strain of the interest she took in the poet's welfare).

It is perhaps slightly unfortunate that the Dylan/Caitlin domestic saga *does* have a certain sub-Joycean feel to it. In its self-centredness, their borrowing and scrounging somehow lack the dimension of heroic recklessness that informs the Joyce/Nora life saga, in its penniless wanderings from Dublin to Trieste, and then through Rome, Zurich and Paris, with plenty of time, apparently, for Joyce to detect that a Triestine manufacturer of paint for warships' hulls is an undiscovered genius – and in due course to present him to the world as the comic novelist Italo Svevo.

A difference is, of course, that Joyce was not above menial toil when the going got tough, as spells teaching English and clerking in a Rome bank attest. Thomas was quite clear that he would not undertake anything that might divert him from his poetry (though as we have seen he allowed himself a flexible conscience in that regard when it came to the film world). Joyce, too, could not write about Ireland without having a healthy distance between him and its Jesuitical soul. For Thomas, Wales was a recurrent necessity.

And as it happened, the involuntary flight back to Wales from the raining down of the V-weapons on southern England in 1944 was a decisive step in Thomas's later career. The New Quay sojourn was not to be a long one. Nor was New Quay Laugharne, with its familiar eccentricities and beguiling conjunction of rivers, but a place of bungalows and retirement homes on a not particularly picturesque stretch of the Cardiganshire coast. But it gave Caitlin the chance to create again, however briefly, that domestic framework for Thomas, without which he was always a prey to destructive influences. It ushered in a period of creativity that was richly to atone for the inactivity of 1941-44 – and which he was never to match again. 'Poem in October', 'In my craft or sullen art', 'A Refusal to Mourn the Death, by Fire, of a Child in London' and 'Fern Hill' are all productions of the months between August 1944 and October 1945. They were to form the eloquent core of the volume *Deaths and Entrances*, which was published in 1946. It was, comprehensively, to answer those – among friends and champions, as well as the cynics who had always held his art to be suspect – who feared that the war years had irrevocably squandered his gift.

But *Deaths and Entrances* was soon to be seen not merely as a case of a volume which happily confirmed the merits of a poet from whom the world had not heard for far too long. It announced that 'After the Funeral' had not been an accident, something awakened solely by the intense memory of a beloved aunt, and afterwards to be laid to sleep again. Its ringing affirmations promise that the poet has left behind for ever the unprofitable inner gnawings of his earlier manner. Thomas here strides with a firm tread in a much more spacious mental and physical landscape than before. This is work which is, in the words of his own prefatory note to the *Collected Poems,* "written for the love of Man and in praise of God".

Deaths and Entrances had originally been planned by Dent for 1945. But in October that year Thomas was still at work on two new poems, one, 'In my craft or sullen art', the other 'Fern Hill', perhaps his most famous single poem. He was adamant with Dent that he wanted the latter to be included in the new volume – and one can see why. Lines from this magnificent elegy for childhood seem utterly appropriate to adorn his commemorative stone in St Paul's Cathedral. Dent gracefully acceded to the wishes of their wayward author, with whom they had not always been well pleased. In the event, both poems were included, 'Fern Hill' as the poem that brought the volume resoundingly to a close.

When the volume was published on 7th February 1946 its author was a man in a high state of nervous tension. Like almost all writers, he pretended an indifference to reviews, but he pored over them obsessively in the privacy of his own study, hating in equal measure, not only criticism, but praise for the 'wrong' reasons. In this instance he need not have worried. *Deaths and Entrances* was both a critical and commercial success. Norman Cameron's review in the *Tribune* summed up the general perception of the advance this book represented on what had gone before it: "Mr Thomas, even in his earliest work, could do 'magnificent things with words'. Now he can do magnificent things with poems."

Whereas so often before Thomas had given the impression that word controlled and modified thought, now, it appeared, a poem took shape in his mind, and he cloaked that impulse in words. As we see from his worksheets, that was not in fact the case. His working methods remained very much the same as they had always been. Nevertheless, the experience of the war (which did, in the end, make something of a 'war poet' of him), and of its frightening capacity virtually to silence him, had unlocked something within him. With the clotted inwardness of gaze locked forever within the Buffalo Notebooks on the other side of the Atlantic, it is as if Thomas has assumed something akin to Blake's "bow of burning gold" and, as it were, taken up his "arrows of desire". There is, as G.S. Fraser has remarked, a "glowing transformation" about these poems.

The book sold well, The first 3,000 copies went in a month, and Dent ordered a reprint of the same number. They also took advantage of a new-found fame, which was now augmented by readings and discussions on the radio, to disinter the unbound sheets of his previous work, and put that on sale again.

9

Deaths and Entrances

Deaths and Entrances is not without its difficulties. But they are not
the kind of difficulties that stall us at the outset in its predecessors,
requiring a fundamental regrouping before we can proceed. It can
(with a certain judicious selectiveness, particularly of its longer
offerings) be read through, as one would hope to be able to browse
in a volume of poetry. That said, the title poem is best passed over. It
was written in August 1940, before the creative drought that was
only ended with the return to Wales in 1944, and seems to belong to
Thomas's previous incarnation. It makes gestures, but attempts no
great affirmations.

It could be regarded as one of Thomas's 'war poems', poems,
that is, written by the civilian who happens to find himself in the
front line. But its allusion to the conflict's impact on the onlooker in
this war is a somewhat oblique one. Three poems – 'Among those
Killed in the Dawn Raid was a Man Aged a Hundred', 'Ceremony
after a Fire Raid' and 'Refusal to Mourn the Death, by Fire, of a
Child in London' – directly confront the experience.

The first of these, too, dates from before the creative 'silence' of
the mid-war years – indeed it seems to be virtually the last poem he
wrote, before turning his back on his craft. It reads like a first,
shocked, but not fully assimilated, reaction to the violence of war.
(It also, one feels, springs from an experience of the bombing of
Swansea, not London.): "When the morning was waking over the
war/He put on his clothes and stepped out and he died ..." This is
Dylan Thomas some considerable way below his best. Even the
rhythm falters in the truly dreadful doggerel of the second line, a
thing extremely rare in Thomas.

It is an index of his inability to make the death of the old man

56

meaningful for us in symbolic terms. The very choice of "a man aged a hundred" is perhaps unfortunate. (One presumes that Thomas had actually heard of this occurrence, and the incongruity of it somehow struck him into versifying it.) But the fact is that most human beings are in their graves long before that age, anyway, and the pity we want to feel simply will not come. "dropped where he loved" introduces another incongruity. Are we meant to imagine that a man of a hundred is still making love – love of a kind that is consummated on the floor in the abandonment of passion? Or does this refer to love, merely in the sense of 'love and charity with thy neighbour?'

Compare it with this, the opening of 'Ceremony after a Fire Raid', the poem Thomas composed next after it – a full 33 months later: "Myselves/The grievers/Grieve .../A child of a few hours .../Charred on the black breast of the grave/The mother dug, and its arms full of fires." The child, of course, makes all the difference. And from the very outset Thomas has enlisted us with him in the ranks of the mourners. A life of a few hours has been violently extinguished while being suckled at its mother's breast. The mother, too, has been incinerated, and her breast is now the child's grave. The punning on "dug", which acts simultaneously as both noun and verb, is a masterly conceit that treads the border of poor taste without falling over it. The mother, in a sense, dug her own child's grave by doing and being what she was at that moment – a young woman suckling her child and being necessarily vulnerable to violent assault in the performance of that act. The notion of the child with "its arms full of fires" conjures up something akin to Shakespeare's "naked new born babe, striding the blast", invoking sensations of awe and pity.

In the poem's second movement, Thomas, now bard – and priest – goes on to invest this scrap of extinguished humanity with a significance that goes far beyond the death of a single individual: "I know not whether/Adam or Eve, the adorned holy bullock/Or the white ewe lamb/Or the chosen virgin .../was the first to die ..." The child's death has become one with the fate of the first human parents as told in Genesis. The "adorned holy bullock" links this 'ceremony' of its death with the classical Greek sacrificial ceremony sketched for us by Keats in 'Ode on a Grecian Urn', with its "heifer lowing at the skies,/And all her silken flanks with garlands drest ..."

The "white ewe lamb" and the "chosen virgin" bring together the Agnus Dei of the Christian requiem mass with the sacrificial virgins of Minoan myth, and, possibly, pre-Christian Celtic sacrifice. All, now, are summed up in the fate of this tiny victim of war, in whose service, too, the poet pledges himself never to be silent.

By the third movement, the poet has passed far beyond grieving to a state of exultation in which the sea itself (always important as a life-bearing element to the shore-dwelling Thomas) is imperiously invoked.

In 'After the Funeral' the poet, as Ann's bard, had called "all the seas to service" in the celebration of her death and life. Now in a passage which hurls together medieval church architecture, church music, urn burial, and the objects of the sacrament, in which, however, both bread and wine seem to have taken on a self-consuming incandescence, he again steps in – like some Poseidon called from the classical Greek pantheon – and conjures the sea to "enter" this shattered and disordered world as the instrument of a final, triumphant apotheosis.

Is Thomas a religious poet? In a sense, yes, but I do not think he is a Christian one. He is utterly at home with the verbal furniture of the Bible and the church liturgy. He was nurtured on it and it is naturally his constant recourse. But he appropriates it to his own purposes. 'God' is not a difficult idea for him. But there is not a scrap of Christian humility in Thomas. He does not, as Hopkins, or before him, Herbert, did, wrestle with God. In such a poem as this he is not asking for intercession for the soul of the slain child. Rather, he effortlessly assumes the mantle of both priest and pantocrator.

I confess to preferring this poem to the widely-admired 'Refusal to Mourn', which was composed in March 1945. It is to be assumed the latter is another reflection on the same death, though of course the incineration of infants in fire raids must have been a common enough wartime occurrence. It does not greatly matter. This is clearly a more muted performance than its predecessor. The title is actually more provocative than the substance of the poem itself. The poet appears to be saying, in the long first sentence that extends over thirteen lines, that from the creation to Judgement Day ("the last light breaking,/And the still hour") there will be no need to mourn the child's death. Only at that latter point will he "let pray the shadow of a sound ... to mourn/The majesty and burning of the child's death".

The two poems do not, of course, have to be taken in conjunction, but there is an inevitable temptation to read them side by side. And this seems to be a retreat from the triumphant assertion of 'Ceremony'. That took us beyond grief and mourning. This brings us back to it. There is no sense of triumphant heavenward flight, here, as there was in 'Ceremony after a Fire Raid'. Instead, with "Deep with the first dead lies London's daughter .../Secret by the unmourning water" we are in the comfortless atmosphere of the Hebrew Sheol. The water, here is "unmourning" – embodied in the Thames which merely flows indifferently by – and not, as in 'Ceremony', the sea whose irresistible agency bears the child's death away on the tide of eternity. The conclusion: "After the first death, there is no other." is a somewhat half-hearted one. The first death equals all subsequent deaths, and unites them in the earth where they lie, making them part of the "grains beyond age". It has a tidy cleverness about it that is not characteristic of Thomas. It might have been written by Auden, Spender or Day Lewis. Somewhere along the line the child's bard has slipped down off that magnificent peak of exaltation to which he ascended in 'Ceremony after a Fire Raid'.

Readers and critics tend to approach the 'Ballad of the Long-Legged Bait' and beat a hasty retreat before its sheer length and its cloudy imagery. In his younger days Thomas had liked to refer to himself as the "Rimbaud of Cwmdonkin Drive". Whether he regarded the 'Ballad', with its salty theme, as a nod towards 'Le Bateau Ivre' is not known. It seems unlikely. Rimbaud was, after all, only 17 when he wrote his poem, and had never seen the sea. Thomas was in his late twenties. For a seaside dweller like him, a fisherman setting off in a boat would be a natural setting for a parable of self-discovery such as this.

Then, again, Rimbaud's celebrated poem is a chaotic dream of total liberation from the constraints of a bourgeois family, school, and the provinces, for which the drunken boat is a perfect vehicle. By contrast, the braver critics have detected a very distinct purpose – and a moral one at that – to Thomas's 'Ballad'.

To Elder Olson the eponymous "Long-Legged Bait", the naked woman who is cast into the sea by the fisherman to be consumed by its denizens, is a desire (also the desires of his own heart) which must be sacrificed to restore the lost Eden. Thus the poem becomes a struggle between Thomas's Welsh puritanism and the natural desires of the flesh.

As expressed in the poem this is certainly not a particularly attractive idea. Lines such as "For we saw him throw to the swift flood/A girl alive with his hooks through her lips" verge on the pornographic. And there is a certain misogynistic relish in "Susannah's drowned by the bearded stream/And no-one stirs at Sheba's side." Two of the great biblical temptresses are eliminated from the fisherman's pilgrimage.

John Ackerman sees the woman as the bait "whereby through the celebration of the flesh, new life and spiritual regeneration is to be obtained". In a New York bar, Dylan Thomas apparently once told an audience that the ballad was about a young man who goes out fishing for fun and games and instead hooks a wife and family – a clearly unreliable testimony, and a mock-rueful comment on his own domestic circumstances.

What is clear is that the poem is far too long and far too confused. Its central section loses all rhythm, sense and interest. The total conviction of the manner in which Thomas read it for a recording would certainly have convinced anyone of its clarity. But as soon as the marvellous voice falls silent, we are left in as great a fog as before.

'Poem in October' is, by contrast, one of the great Dylan Thomas 'favourites' and always crops up in anthologies. That popularity undoubtedly owes much to its immediate intelligibility. Thomas described it to Vernon Watkins as a "Laugharne poem: the first place poem I've written". In the opening lines: "It was my thirtieth year to heaven/Woke to my hearing from harbour and neighbour wood/And the mussel pooled and the heron/Priested shore" we are very much in the country of (the as-yet unwritten, but certainly conceived) *Under Milk Wood*. In our passage through Thomas's oeuvre so far, we have become so used to wrestling meaning from his images, that it might, again, seem a curmudgeonly complaint that we seem almost not to have *enough* work to do here. Yet there is a strange lack of intensity in the "water praying and call of seagull and rook/And the knock of sailing boats on the net webbed wall". Apart from the "praying" water – a less effective image than the "heron/Priested shore" – it is completely lacking in metaphorical life. It might almost be a landscape description by a tiro aiming at "poetical" prose.

By stanza three "A springful of larks in a rolling/Cloud and the roadside bushes brimming with whistling/Blackbirds ..." a resolute benignity of gaze has set in, threatening to kill off our interest as the poem charts its linear path through a series of itemized sights and sounds.

The tone changes and the poem's real preoccupations are revealed when, at the end of the next stanza "... the weather turned around." The mood changes. The true goal of this morning's setting-out is now revealed. Vivid memories of childhood crowd in on him. The poem suddenly discovers a metaphorical dimension, though it is, by Thomas's standards, a weakly-enough articulated one. We have to let "parables of sunlight" go by us as somehow suggesting a mother's storytelling on a sunlit walk, rather than being able to tease a more resounding meaning from it. The "green" chapels – those of his youth of far-off memory – may also double as, or merely be intended to suggest, the mysterious "Grene Chapel" of Gawain's tryst with the Green Knight.

Nevertheless, these memories buoy him up. He recalls that Thomas the boy "In the listening/Summertime of the dead whispered the truth of his joy" And – as a man for so long cut off from that 'truth' embodied in the sources of his poetic inspiration – he is able to end his birthday poem with the, we think optimistic, supplication "O may my heart's truth/still be sung/On this high hill in a year's turning." The supplication is admittedly, a somewhat easily-purchased one. There is a sense, in this somewhat perfunctory excursion back into childhood, that something has not been properly worked out.

We have only to consider the celebrated opening of 'Fern Hill' to feel the difference. Quite apart from anything else, the verse scheme looks as if it has shaped itself under the irresistible pressure of thought. If one quoted 'Poem in October' aloud, from memory and then wrote it down, one might find oneself end-stopping the lines very differently from the way Thomas has set them out. Here, there is a certain inevitability – though, as we always know with Thomas, that is achieved only through the painstaking application of his craft.

The energy of Thomas's splendid rhythm aside, there is an immediate engagement with the subject that was only tentatively achieved in 'Poem in October'. Weak nostalgia is replaced with a powerful rapture of recollection. Images of a farm childhood with its tilth, its harvest and its fruit trees – all "green" – swarm in on the poet.

We see him in the first stanza, riding on top of a farm cart which is bringing in the harvest from the fields. He is "prince of the apple towns", as the laden vehicle with its high load, squeezes under the branches of an orchard on its way into the rickyard, strewing among its twigs wisps, plucked from its cargo of barley sheaves, and the daisies that have become mixed with them in the process of reaping. The "windfall light" may refer to apples that are knocked down in this passage, combined, as Thomas so often likes to do, with a second idea, that the very summer's light of that day, was itself a rare gift.

It has become almost a commonplace to compare the visionary rapture of Thomas in this poem, with that of Traherne or Vaughan. This is highly misleading. To Thomas, yes, nature is holy. Yet we are never sure, here, that Heaven shares that conviction – that, in Blake's words, "Eternity is in love with the productions of time". The two seem at odds with each other. The vision is touched with a powerful sense of mortality. The short lines "Time let me hail and climb" and "Time let me play and be" are like hammer blows which remind the poet, as surely as those that will drive the nails into his coffin, that life is on a short lease.

Though there is recurrent religious imagery throughout the remainder of the poem: "the sabbath rang slowly"; "the pebbles of the holy streams"; "it was Adam and maiden"; "the fields of praise", it is "time" who holds the cards in this Garden of Eden, toying, though they do not know it, with the young lives of Fern Hill Farm. And at the end, time, like some malevolent cosmic Pied Piper, leads his young charges out of, not into, grace.

The conclusion of the poem seems to draw back from this sombre metaphysical standpoint. True, at the end the poet is still in thrall to time: "Oh as I was young and easy in the mercy of his means,/Time held me green and dying/Though I sang in my chains like the sea." The precise interpretation of this will depend on whether we take the word "though" as the conjunction 'although', or give it the sense of 'and yet'. If the former, then the poet simply sings blindly – if bravely – as he goes into the darkness, oblivious to his fate. If the latter, then we are in the presence of some sort of a struggle against the inevitability of his fate. Aware of what is in store, the poet sings defiance in his chains. He is not finished yet. Furthermore he sees himself and his song-making in terms of the sea, that – always for Thomas – source of life-giving powers. There is an exhilarating feeling of carelessness as to the outcome, of a sense that the poet, and this visionary re-creation of his childhood with which he has enthralled us, yet have their valued place in the eternal order of things.

10

The Dying of the Light

The eight years of life remaining to Thomas after the publication of *Deaths and Entrances* make a dreary chronicle. It is a constant begging and scrounging amid penury, gypsy wanderings, rising alcoholism, an increasingly inharmonious marriage and finally the fatal four tours to America. And they were years of declining creativity. Between 1946 and 1953 he wrote only seven poems, and one of those was the prologue to the *Collected Poems*, without which the volume could live quite comfortably.

Yet among the other six poems are four which are reckoned to be among his finest: 'Over Sir John's hill', 'In the White Giant's Thigh', 'Do not go gentle into that good night' and 'Poem on his Birthday'. And there is of course the much-loved play for voices *Under Milk Wood*.

Many explanations have been given for the parlous state of Thomas's finances throughout this period. Yet it still seems extraordinary that one of Britain's most famous poets should have been constantly languishing in a state of such indigence. Why was he so poor? Granted, the tax authorities were by now taking an unhealthy interest in him, now that he was a proven money earner. But could not Dent, now surely in the confident expectation of recouping well from him, have advanced him some sort of income (as an American publisher had earlier), or at least some accountancy advice? Certainly his agent David Higham appears to have tried to shield him from the taxman, engaging an accountant to work out a plan by which the Inland Revenue's demands might be mitigated on a basis of regular payments. None of this was, of course, easy, given that Thomas had never kept any records of his receipts and had not paid any tax from the beginning of his earning life.

Is Thomas, then, to be pitied in this pinch? Or was he so utterly feckless that no amounts of money would not have run through his hands? Was he really capable of drinking away everything he earned? Was he in New York recklessly standing drinks for hangers-on which it ought to have been his position, as the famous poet, to have received? Certainly we know he developed an appetite for taking taxis over long distances when the mood took him. And those who knew him recall a predilection for the betting shop. But none of these things, taken either separately or together, would seem to account for an existence led on the borders of absolute penury for eight long years.

Would it have made any difference to his production of poetry had he not had to write scripts for films and broadcasts to make a living? A quintessentially Romantic poet of the type traditionally not noted for long life, had he in fact said all that he had to say? We know he is on record as lamenting at one point to the critic John Davenport: "I can't go on. I've already had twice as much of it as Keats." Did he know within himself that in his public broadcasts, talks, essays and even the prodigious effort that went into the first production of *Under Milk Wood* in 1952, he was, in fact saying good-bye to his genius and filling what should have been hours devoted to poetry with the productions of mere talent?

Thomas and Caitlin returned from Cardiganshire to London in the autumn of 1945 to begin an existence of wretched shiftlessness. As we have seen, Margaret Taylor took the whole family on board and in March 1946 let them have the use of a summer house in the grounds of their own house at Oxford, where A.J.P. Taylor was now a Fellow of Magdalen. The house had never been intended to house a family of four, and when Thomas peremptorily demanded a caravan, to give him peace and quiet so that he could write, she obliged him with that, too. His wartime film-script work had by this time come to an end. But there was a living to be made at the BBC where the new 'intellectual' Third Programme provided the nation with a diet of the arts, which included copious poetry and drama readings. Thomas's magnificent reading voice made him much in demand – and greatly added to his reputation even among those who might not normally read much poetry.

Caitlin, again, regarded this as a betrayal of himself. The dramatis persona of the broadcasting studio so often could not stop acting in the pub afterwards. It was a magnificent show for those who liked hanging in with the famous poet. For her, if she happened to be present, it was simply a prostitution of his genius. She also hated being dependent on Margaret Taylor's charity. She not unnaturally assumed the interest that the don's wife took in Thomas's welfare had a motive other than the desire merely to be of service to genius, and this led to furious rows, first with Thomas, and then with Margaret.

Then, in the spring of 1947 he was awarded a travelling scholarship by the Authors' Society. This he very largely owed to Edith Sitwell who, like Margaret Taylor, had stayed loyal to her first enthusiasm and continued to exert herself on his behalf. On the advice of various friends, Thomas decided to go with his family to Italy, traditionally the overseas sojourn for an English man of letters. The idea appealed doubly, in an English winter which had been the harshest in living memory. Two years after the end of the war there seemed to be no end in sight to the economic austerity that held the country in its grip.

Yet the six months' stay, in which they were accompanied by Caitlin's sister Brigid and her child, first in a villa above Florence and then on the isle of Elba when the blistering heat of the Tuscan countryside became too much for Thomas, was not a success. Thomas might have foreseen this. He already had a strong premonition that he was not the stuff, either physically or mentally, of which 'Mediterranean man' is compounded. In 1938 Lawrence Durrell, then an admirer of Thomas's work, had invited him and Caitlin to join him on Corfu. Thomas had replied: "If I went to the sun I'd just sit in the sun; that would be very pleasant but I'm not doing it."

The stay in Italy turned out to be one of creative frustration. He found the heat oppressive and could get no work done in the afternoon, his preferred time of the day for writing. His Italian was rudimentary and there could be little meaningful contact with those deputations of Florence intelligentsia who occasionally beat a path to the Villa de Becaro at Mosciano. To get into Florence where he might meet them in the cool of a bar, involved hiring a horse and trap to Scandicci and then taking a crowded tram in the heat of the day down into Florence, a jolting half-hour ride. To abbreviate this ordeal by the hire of a car cost the equivalent of 30 shillings, a meaningless sum at this distance, unless one thinks of it as one-and-a-half times the daily wage of a farm labourer in the England of those days.

The drinking regime, too, did not suit Thomas the beer drinker. Italian beer, thin stuff at best even today, was in those days an unpalatable, faintly sulphurous-tasting, brew that Thomas found quite impossible to get down him. As a result he drank wine. But he drank it as if it had been beer – a procedure fatal to any attempt to stay awake and write in the hot sun. The wine from the local cantina, was, anyway, in those postwar times before some standards were introduced into production, harsh and acidic. Drunk in volume it wrought havoc on a digestive system that was already beginning to collapse under the weight of alcohol with which it was daily abused. The other available recourse, sticky-sweet Italian brandy, made for a lethal cocktail when drunk in tandem with wine.

Desperately homesick, Thomas found himself tuning in to long-wave radio and listening to the cricket commentaries of his old friend, and the producer of many of his BBC talks, John Arlott, from Trent Bridge and Lords. Entertaining and informative though the scene-painting of that inimitable analyst of the game always was, there is something incongruous in the notion of one of England's finest contemporary writers, gifted the Grand Tour to Florence, having, as a mental resource, to rely on words emanating, via a radio, from an English cricket ground.

By contrast, Caitlin found herself hugely enjoying the Mediterranean ambience. A more genuinely earthy individual than Thomas, she worshipped light and sun. She blossomed in the intoxicating heat and the wild-flower scents of the Tuscan countryside. And she loved the guilt-free importunings of the Italian male.

In the end the Italian experience was not an unmitigated disaster for Thomas. At Mosciano he completed 'In Country Sleep', the first of that final clutch of poems which appeared in America in a volume of that title in February 1952 and were included in the *Collected Poems* published in England later that year. It was intended as one movement of a poem on epic scale, to be entitled 'In Country Heaven'.

In September 1950 Thomas was to describe his intentions for this in a radio talk (later printed as the essay 'Three Poems' in the prose collection *Quite Early One Morning*). By that time Thomas had also completed 'Over Sir John's hill' and 'In the White Giant's Thigh', though he admitted that he had little idea of where the last, at least would fit into the overall scheme of the epic.

In his own words: "The godhead, the author, the milky-way farmer, the first cause, architect ... weeps whenever outside that state of being called his country, one of his worlds drops dead" This is of course a radio talk. Delivered in Thomas's booming voice, its jumble of assertions seemed doubtless to promise great things. But it is difficult in retrospect to see, for example, where 'Over Sir John's hill', which was, apparently, to have opened this great project, really fits into this scheme, magnificent though it is as an individual poem. The truth is that Thomas was a poet of the short lyric burst. He may (possibly under the influence of his readings from Milton for the BBC – "first cause", certainly harks back to the opening of *Paradise Lost*) have fancied himself as capable of epic. But his methods of composition were simply alien to the formal organisation necessary to a long, narrative poem. 'In Country Heaven' never materialised. But we are grateful for its three constituents.

By July, Thomas had had enough of the heat of inland Tuscany, and moved with his troop of incumbents to Rio Marina, a small fishing port on the eastern coast of Elba. It was just as hot there, but there were occasional relieving breezes at dawn and dusk, and the children at least could go in the sea.

While Thomas, sick in mind and body, did absolutely nothing except slake his thirst with alcohol, Caitlin dallied with the, considerably younger, owner of their hotel. Whether this flirtation, under Thomas's nose, was consummated at that time is impossible to say. A year after Thomas's death in 1953, Caitlin was to return to Elba and a brief fling with the man, a strong, silent type, whose uncomplicated ardour appealed to her after the self-scarifying neuroses of her husband.

Italy, where Thomas had only gone to spend a grant on the say-so of friends, was to provide her with a future in an ambience as unlike that of Wales as can be imagined. There was to be a further affair, with a much younger fisherman on the isle of Procida in the Bay of

Naples. This lasted some time before she eventually, in 1957, found Rome and, in the Sicilian Giuseppe Fazio, a permanent partner and the father of her fourth child.

But for now, the Elba interlude was to be the affair of a mere fortnight. Thomas's powers of begging and borrowing could do nothing to extend it – and he was anyway heartily sick of the place. He had already corresponded with Margaret Taylor. That willing patron was on hand with another refuge for the family when they returned to England in August. This was a farmhouse in the village of South Leigh in Oxfordshire, a ramshackle place without a bathroom or even a proper lavatory. So that her poet should not be inconvenienced by the strains of domestic life in such a place, Mrs Taylor had his caravan towed there from Oxford to enable him to work unhindered.

It was a hopeless situation. Thomas who, to Caitlin's fury, had taken more screen-writing work, this time with Gainsborough films, spent much of the time travelling between South Leigh and London, either sleeping there after a night's drinking, or returning at night using taxis they could not afford.

The strains of such an existence were finally compounded by the terminal illness of his father, who had cancer, and his mother who seriously injured her leg in a fall. After spending some time with his sister and her husband (who were on the verge of leaving England to live abroad) both parents were eventually transported to South Leigh. There, and afterwards in Laugharne, they were effectively to be dependent on Thomas (which in practical terms meant Caitlin) for their support.

In May 1949 Thomas made what was to be his last house move. Again, Margaret Taylor was his benefactor. Selling South Leigh, she bought what was shortly to become famous as the Boat House at Laugharne. The idea was that he should pay her a modest rent for it (which he seldom did). At the same time she organised a cottage for his parents, nearby. Caitlin, in the meantime, was heavily pregnant with their third child while this move was being undertaken. Their second son, Colm was born in Laugharne in July.

This last move provided the soil for a final flowering of Thomas's genius. True, he had only five more poems (six, if we count the Prologue to the *Collected Poems*) in him. Yet the first of these, 'Over

69

Sir John's hill' is steeped in the topography and the waterbirds of Laugharne and its estuary. It must, in spite of the many drafts we know it to have been through, have been written with an uncharacteristic fluency – and velocity – for it to be ready for publication, in the very month of his arrival, in *Botteghe Oscure,* a literary periodical edited in Rome by a wealthy American, Marguerite Caetani, whom Thomas had previously met in London. She became, effectively, in her frequent willingness to advance money for projects that never materialized, another Thomas patroness.

This period after the return to Laugharne and before the American tours gave Caitlin the last months of domestic happiness she was to know. She had her man in a place where she could construct a domestic framework round his working day. And the drinking – in which she ever more freely participated – meant, at least, the manageable beers among the locals at Brown's Hotel.

The idea of America as a place once and for all to make his fortune had been working strongly on Thomas since his first return to London at the end of the war. A visit (only his second overseas venture) to Czechoslovakia, as a guest of its Communist government and writer's union proved something of an impediment. With the palpable onset of the Cold War, the US authorities were going through a virulent anti-Communist purge of all shades of left-wing sentiment among America's own authors. (This paranoia hit particularly hard in Hollywood where some of the best-known names in screenwriting fell victim to the witch-hunts of the now notorious Senator Joseph McCarthy and the House un-American activities Committee, and had their careers ruined).

Thomas had, of course, not a scrap of doctrinal socialism in his creative makeup, beyond a woolly notion that anything that was to the benefit of the downtrodden working man of the kind among whom he had grown up was basically a 'good thing'. The idea of the proletariat's "owning the means of production" was a high-sounding notion with which he could have no quarrel. His Czech hosts, newly under the heel of their Soviet masters, were not likely to divulge to him the brutal means by which this wholesome manifesto was actually enforced, nor the iron ideological constraints under which their writers operated.

First and foremost, Thomas needed an American sponsor. One was now at hand in the person of John Malcolm Brinnin, a poet who admired his work, but had lacked any kind of position from which to be able to help him. Now, in the same month in which Thomas and family moved into the Boat House, Brinnin was appointed director of the Poetry Center of the Young Men's and Young Women's Hebrew Association (YM-YWHA) in New York. He immediately dispatched a letter to Laugharne, suggesting that Thomas might like to come to America for a series of poetry readings. Thomas replied with – for him – alacrity, proposing the visit for early the following year.

Thus, from this somewhat unlikely sounding source, came the suggestion that was potently to alter the course of Thomas's remaining life.

It is easy to laugh at Brinnin. He was a bit of a stuffed shirt, who when faced with a man like Thomas in his roaring drunk mode was completely at a loss. There is much self-justification in his book *Dylan Thomas in America* (1956) of his handling of the relationship with his formidable guest. And he is particularly obtuse in his surprise that Caitlin, who accompanied Thomas on the second of his four tours, regarded him as the enemy of everything Thomas should have been striving for at that point. (She was to regard him as a worse 'seducer' than Donald Taylor had been at Strand Films.) Yet Brinnin's account remains the most valuable one we have of the experience, and demonstrates that Brinnin, an essentially kindly man, had his heart in the right place.

His generous praise of the tours, delivered in a radio broadcast, suggests that they were by no means entirely the "expense of spirit in a waste of shame" they have commonly been represented as. Their impact was widespread and lasting. A rising generation of Beat Poets, led by Allen Ginsburg, was to learn lessons from them about new ways of making poetry.

Apart from one reading he failed to make, at Tulane University, New Orleans, in 1953, Thomas surprised audiences, some of whom might have seen him in a state of disorder at a party only an hour previously, with his disciplined dedication to these readings. Time after time, he pulled himself together from a state of seemingly irretrievable intoxication that terrified his hosts, straightened his bow tie and walked out on to the stage to speak lines from Yeats, Auden and other contemporaries as a preface to the finest of his own work delivered in that marvellous baritone voice.

And whatever else his faults, it is to Brinnin's eternal credit that he stuck with his almost impossible visitor. In the process he drove himself well-nigh mad and ill with worry, but he arranged not only the promised readings but enabled Thomas through his own wide circle, to make a host of other contacts, of the sort that eventually led to the first full performance of *Under Milk Wood* in New York in May 1953. The BBC, whose relationship with the poet had become increasingly acrimonious since his failing to deliver a promised manuscript for a production of *Peer Gynt*, had to wait until January 1954 for its first broadcast.

Brinnin perceived through the wilfully uncontrollable behaviour, as perhaps many more acute sensibilities did not at that time, that some serious realization was at work in Thomas: "All my sense, then, as it is now, was that the term of the roaring boy was over, and that the means by which Dylan might continue to grow wise were no longer in his possession ..." The tour of 1950 lasted from February to June. It was followed by more than a year at home (broken by a trip to Persia for an abortive film for the Anglo-Iranian oil company) in which, at Laugharne, he was able between September 1950 and the summer of 1951, effectively to finish all the poems we have (save, that is for the Prologue, which held up the publication of the *Collected Poems*, much as 'Fern Hill' had delayed that of *Deaths and Entrances*).

In 1952 there was another tour, which was none the more successful for Caitlin's insisting on going with him. To her these tours were occasions "only for flattery, idleness and infidelity". (Margaret Taylor had been assiduous in informing her about the one more than usually resounding instance of the last, which had the beloved object – a senior magazine executive – actually pursuing Thomas to London on his return.) Tour number two did not benefit from Caitlin's cloudy presence on the flanks of whatever knot of admirers might gather round Thomas of an evening. From there she tried to keep a sharp lookout against the possibility of his being made away with by some 'ardent', as he styled these female groupies, under her very nose.

In such circumstances it is seldom any consolation – though men perennially seem to think it is – for a woman to be assured that her man was 'too drunk', 'didn't know what he was doing' and that it 'all meant nothing'. Indeed, it is generally quite the reverse. A woman is apt to divine that sexual infidelity arising purely from an excess of drink is liable to be repeated more often than that which has involved some expense of genuine emotion. In the last, and most vitriolic, of her accounts of her marriage to Thomas, *Double Drink Story*, published posthumously in 1998, Caitlin has given a vivid impression of her sense of humiliation.

This wretched experience came to an end in May 1952. Back in Laugharne Dylan worked frantically on the Prologue for the impending *Collected Poems*. As he apologized to E.F. Bozman at Dent, in the letter of September 1952 which eventually accompanied the manuscript: "The Prologue is in two verses – in my manuscript, a verse to a page – of 51 lines each. And the second verse rhymes backward with the first. The first & last lines of the poem rhyme … Why I acrosticked myself like this, don't ask me." To his bitter disappointment, when he read the Prologue to Louis MacNeice, that exquisitely-tuned poetic ear did not detect the device with which Thomas had wrestled for so long.

Collected Poems 1934-1952 appeared exactly two months after the letter to Bozman, on 10th November 1952. The reviews constituted an almost universal acclamation. In *The Sunday Times* Cyril Connolly hailed him as "unique"; for *The Observer* Philip Toynbee's verdict was that he was the "greatest living poet". Thomas's own favourite review was that by Stephen Spender, to whom he took the trouble to write a letter thanking his fellow poet for having praised him, above all, for the 'right' reasons.

Commercially the book was a massive success. Ten thousand copies were sold in the first year alone, and this figure was to be hugely augmented by its appearance, to an even greater fanfare, in New York the following March. In America recordings of his readings were by now enjoying very large sales, too. And yet, all this was somehow too late for Thomas. Caitlin was to become a rich woman almost in the first year of her widowhood, but in the immediate term, financial humiliation and personal sorrow beat in on her husband and continually eroded his will to continue. Their son Llewelyn had to be removed from school for the non-payment of his fees; the Inland

Revenue pursued him for £1,900 tax, which they deemed payable on his American earnings. Even the welfare state was after him for £50 for unpaid National Insurance stamps.

Then, within a month of the publication of *Collected Poems*, his father, to whom he had grown closer down the years, died of his cancer. This was a bitter blow to Thomas, who, in his psychologically fragile state was not able to protect himself by the show of cynicism he had staged on the death of his aunt Annie, 20 years before. News of his sister's death, in India the following April, was not a comparable blow, but it added to the sense that a past was being systematically extinguished, and that ahead lay only mortality.

In the meantime, Margaret Taylor, whose marriage had by that time become a victim to her infatuation with Thomas, threatened to turn her tenants out of the Boat House unless some rent was paid. Pleading to a sceptical Caitlin that another American tour was needed to restore their financial position, Thomas set off again for the States in April 1953.

The tour was of a far more sensible duration than its lengthy predecessors – two months – and had its successes for Thomas in creative, as well as performing terms. *Under Milk Wood* was given a solo performance by him at Harvard on 3rd May 1953, and had its first full performance by a cast of actors – which included Thomas – at the YM-YWHA Poetry Center on 14th May. These performances kept him thinking, writing and rewriting, since he was refining the concept before each of them – and continued to do so afterwards.

He owed a good deal of the success of the Poetry Center performance to Brinnin's assistant there, Liz Reitell, a superficially feisty, though at bottom vulnerable, woman who aimed to take him in hand, organising his schedule of work, sharing his bed at times and trying, ultimately unsuccessfully, to moderate his drinking. Nevertheless, within the remit of damage limitation, she was basically 'good' for him at that time. At least they both had the same aim, to make *Under Milk Wood* work, and she played her part in that end, shutting her eyes to much else.

Another, and very exciting, project, mooted during this visit, was the prospect of collaborating with Stravinsky on an opera to be commissioned by Boston University. Thomas was at first overawed by the prospect of writing a libretto for so famous a personage and artist. But when he met the composer in Boston, he was, in spite of his nerves, able to give a good account of the theme he had in mind. It was to be a story, set in the aftermath of a nuclear catastrophe, of the rediscovery and redemption of the world. Thomas promised concrete ideas and simple language, stripped of his normal tendency to the ornately symbolic.

Stravinsky listened intently, warming to the notion and instinctively liking its impassioned expositor. They parted on terms of enthusiastic desire for a co-operation along the lines of Thomas's idea. Stravinsky told the poet he hoped to see him in America later in the year, and went home to his house in Hollywood. There, he had an extension built for the accommodation of his expected guest. Thomas returned to Laugharne in June.

The collaboration was never to be. In September Boston University suddenly withdrew their sponsorship. Stravinsky had little doubt that he could raise finance from another source, and continued to consider their project as being very much alive. But that was no help to a man living, as Thomas then was, in desperate need. The advance from Boston that might have relieved his pressing debts was, suddenly, struck from his grasp.

America, still a source of ready income from readings, beckoned irresistibly once more. In spite of the objections, now, of Brinnin, who on a visit for the first time to Laugharne could see that Thomas was a sick man, and urged a period of recuperation, in October he journeyed there for the last time.

On 20th October 1953 he arrived by air in New York, where he was met, and immediately taken charge of by Liz Reitell. Her aim, both for his sake and for that of her own job, was a performance of a finally revised version of *Under Milk Wood* at the YM-YWHA Poetry Center. It might be said that it was achieved in spite of her assiduous watch over him. The performance and a few talks and readings were, miraculously, given. But this time, in spite of her undoubted devotion, she could not separate Thomas from drink – or even other women – when her weary back was turned. With the alcoholic's classic cunning he was always able to evade the caring watchful eye for a moment and disappear. When finally run to earth in a bar, however soon afterwards, he would have reduced himself to the state of a skidrow denizen, of blotched complexion, sweaty linen and a bad breath.

Thomas's various biographers have, with the best of motives, attempted to ascribe his death to a well-meaning but wrong-headed administration of drugs by injection under medical supervision. As an explanation it is not required. Thomas's last remark to Reitell, the famous, "I've had 18 straight whiskies. I think that's a record", may well be an exaggeration. (As a younger man he had once boasted of drinking an impossible 40 pints in an evening.) By this stage no such colossal dosage of alcohol in one session was necessary finally to overwhelm the system of a man who had been systematically abusing it since the beginning of the war.

After this drinking bout Thomas took to his bed and eventually fell into a coma. He was transferred to St Vincent's hospital where, after lingering for a few days, he died on 9th November 1953, barely a fortnight after his 39th birthday. John Malcolm Brinnin's immediate reaction was to telephone the "headquarters of the British delegation to the UN". So famous had the erstwhile Rimbaud of Cwmdonkin Drive become.

From New York the news of his death was broadcast to a shocked world. In California, Stravinsky, waiting for a wire from Thomas which would announce their continued collaboration, received one of a very different sort. He recalled: "All I could do was to cry."

11

Collected Poems 1934-1952

There are, then, only six poems, seven if we include the Prologue, to be considered extra to Thomas's extant œuvre, as we approach the *Collected Poems*. And these six had been published in the US in a volume entitled *In Country Sleep*, nine months before their appearance in *Collected Poems 1934-1952* in the UK.

Is there a legitimate reluctance to consider the Prologue among Thomas's 'true' poems? I think so. For one thing it has about it something of the atmosphere of the 'occasional' poem, in the sense that 'After the funeral' or 'Do not go gentle ...' do not. They are strong outpourings of feeling in reaction to events – in the case of the death of Aunt Annie, one occurring many years before, but only now being felt in its true significance.

The occasion the Prologue celebrates is, of course, the sending forth of his book into the world. It is a custom, neglected by modern poets but much used from the Middle Ages up to and into the 17th century. It is a genre that often produces poems of charm and wit – Herrick's injunctions to his poems, and their potential readers are hilariously funny – but seldom of great stature.

The Prologue was written to do a job, and does it effectively enough. But it seems to me to inhabit a plane of inspiration that is some way below that of 'In the White Giant's Thigh', or 'Poem on his Birthday'. Of course it was actually the last poem Thomas finished, almost a year after its immediate predecessor, 'Poem on his Birthday', which is a product of the summer of 1951. Yet we can see that, in spirit, 'Poem on his Birthday' was really the last poem, the final outpouring of his genius and his farewell to it.

The Prologue is not so much a poem as a poetic exercise. In it, it seems to me, Thomas has already put that genius behind him. There is less of the poems of the late flowering, than of the poetic prose of *Under Milk Wood*, in: "In my seashaken house/On a breakneck of rocks/Tangled with chirrup and fruit,/Froth, flute, fin and quill" Well, one feels, Thomas could continue in this vein for hours. He has been deploying this sort of poetic facility all his creative life. But it seems to me that he has never deployed it to less purpose than he does here. The effect is of a – not very well executed – 17th century still life of the type that is cluttered with game-birds, hares and the odd lobster. The imagery is inert. In fact there is almost nothing here that qualifies as imagery in the terms we expect it of Thomas. Much of it is just a list. "Torrent salmon sun", "seashaken house" , "Gulls, pipers, cockles, and sails", etc. have none of Thomas's usual metaphorical density. Nothing is moving, either in terms of the observed scene or the poet's psychological reading of it.

The closing greeting to the animal inhabitants of this landscape: "Ahoy, old sea-legged fox,/Tom tit and Dai mouse!" has a certain charm about it. But it is charm that relies shamelessly on its 'Welshness', and has nothing to do with the visceral and spiritual relationship Thomas has with the natural world when he is in his profounder mood.

When at the outset of his career, Thomas, in 'Especially when the October wind', unfolded for us the map of his preoccupations, he was able to do so in a language rich with metaphor and intriguing with promise. Here, there is nothing we have not had from him before, and had done much better.

Of the three poems that were to form part of the epic 'In Country Heaven' the first composed was 'In Country Sleep'. It is by far the least satisfactory of the three. It has its moments of power, but they struggle to free themselves from the general prolixity. Few critics have attempted seriously to unravel it from beginning to end.

It is addressed to "my girl". It is not clear whether this is a daughter, or lover, though she may be either or both at times. (The poem has been mentioned in the same breath as Yeats's 'Prayer for my Daughter', though there is scant similarity.) The poet commends his girl to the protection of a benign nature: "Sleep, good, for ever, slow and deep, spelled rare and wise,/My girl ranging the night ..." This might be to a daughter – though surely a somewhat mature one to be addressed in the terms the poet does? He assures her that no sexual threat is to be apprehended in the form either of farm people or their animal charges suddenly turning monster (as they sometimes do in fairy tales). Later, the tone becomes more sombre. Assurance turns to urgent injunction. A feeling of sexual obsession is intensified in: "Oh he/Comes designed to my love to steal not her tide raking/ Wound …/But her faith …" The imagery has become powerfully neurotic and disturbing. Though the poet assures his love that she is not, in fact, to be violated, the terms in which he envisages such an eventuality are too potent to give his assurance much conviction. "Tideraking wound" is 'Eve's wound', possibly thought of here as being broken into during menstruation, since "tideraking" irresistibly evokes the moon-governed rhythms of a woman's body, an enthralment she shares with the sea. The whole is dominated by such manifest sexual anxiety over the mere possibility of his love's being desecrated that the final 'resolution' of: "And you shall wake, from country sleep …/Your faith as deathless as the outcry of the ruled sun." simply evaporates beside it. The haven of "faith" in which the poet wants us to envisage the woman dwelling at the end seems too weakly achieved, the whole arrival not enough striven-for, to carry the intended conviction.

But the foregoing analysis is based on an alighting on the poem's moments of greatest intelligibility. In between lie passages where no meaning can be adduced. 'In Country Sleep' is a long poem, and Thomas is not good at long poems, as 'Ballad of the Long-Legged Bait' attests. His 'thought', such as it was, tended to spring from his head already cloaked in powerful images. It was not a process on which to build the exposition of a philosophy.

'Over Sir John's hill' is a very different proposition. A recognizably 'Laugharne' poem, it owes something of its immense appeal for visitors to that singular town, to the fact that the hill of its title and the waters that surround it can be seen and savoured (though Thomas has changed the name of the river that laps Sir John's hill from Taf to Towy – which is the next stream along – a poetic licence one cannot complain of). But a recognition of its qualities as a poem does not depend on a knowledge of any of this: "Over Sir John's hill,/The hawk on fire hangs still …/And gallows, up the rays of his eyes the small birds of the bay/And the shrill child's play". The birds, here, are made to stand as a metaphor for flawed humanity. (The link between them and us, the human beings, is made quite clearly in the lines in which the "birds of the bay" are equated with "the shrill child's play".) The birds (and we) are young, innocent, tending to gauche. Thomas's god is impersonated by the hawk, who surveys the scene from the heavens and chooses his moment to strike. This is not a loving god, but one of the type of William Blake's Urizen, an authoritarian and judgmental deity, and one given to seeing his relationship with the creation in terms of chastisement.

Thomas, Aesop-like, the recorder of this fable, and the heron, as always, a 'holy' being, lament together over what they see to be inevitable – the punishment of birds/Man for their shortcomings: "We grieve as the blithe birds, never again, leave shingle and elm,/ The heron and I,"

At first they can only sorrow for the birds. Then, like priests, they intercede with the hawk/God for mercy. Later "Who marks the sparrows hail" is a clear reminder to God that, in another, and less severe, mood he is the deity who also, in the words of the hymn, "sees the meanest sparrow fall unnoticed in the street".

Thomas the bard had promised us, in his poetic youth, that he would interpret to us the voice of the trees and the water's speeches. Here, something less in confidence and assurance, he is nevertheless, one with the heron, in feeling that his compassionate grief for humanity will have some value in the eyes of the hawk's presiding and vengefully-inclined deity.

The effectiveness of the theological 'argument' lies in the effortless fusion of a liturgical vocabulary, with the vividly evoked sights and sounds of the natural world. The overall effect is undoubtedly powerfully religious. But it is so in a sense that has nothing to do with formalised Christianity.

Thomas placed 'In the White Giant's Thigh' at the end of *Collected Poems, 1934-1952*. It was not his last poem, but the choice implies he felt it to be his best. Certainly, it seems to express more completely than anything else Thomas wrote, his powerful conviction of the eternal value – whether God cares or not – of humanity's indomitable desires, magnificent procreative urges, and resolute day-to-day striving.

The opening appears to combine two landscapes: "Through throats where many rivers meet, the curlews cry,/Under the conceiving moon, on the high chalk hill," The white giant of the title is clearly the Cerne Abbas Giant, the huge phallic figure carved into a chalk escarpment of the North Dorset Downs. The "cudgelling, hacked/ Hill", which comes in later, clearly refers to this carving process and to the club the figure carries, which complements its huge, erect penis. Thomas's walk within its thighs evokes local legend which has it that sexual intercourse enacted on the grass there ensures fecundity.

This is not to say that Thomas has suddenly translated the heart-land of his concerns to Dorset (which he would have known well enough from his and Caitlin's sojourns with her mother in Ringwood). The women of the poem must be Welsh. They plead in the "waded bay", whose waters lap the Laugharne Sands, for ejaculated semen to enter and inseminate them. For this they yearn "with tongues of curlews", those beautiful wading birds of plaintive and passionate utterance, which inhabit the bay's mud flats at low tide. Indeed the very opening line with its "many rivers meet" suggests inescapably the confluence of the rivers Taf, Towy and Gwendraeth in the estuary Thomas daily saw from his writing shed above the Boat House.

The opening celebrates sexual activity in a manner that would have been totally inconceivable for the little-more-than-adolescent Thomas of "If I were tickled by the rub of love," who recoiled in disgust from the whole idea of the procreative consequences of copulation. Woman, who was treated in that poem as a thief of man's precious seed, is now hymned in the urgency of her desire for conception. And although "the names on their weed grown stones are rained away" – i.e. the women are long dead and the memory of them is obliterated by the elements from their gravestones – their acts, as the mothers of generations, have ensured for them immortality as long as humanity exists to celebrate them.

Thomas's vision here is of the organic unity of nature, which he celebrates exultantly as he elaborates his theme. The women are envisaged at their lovemaking, "Petticoats galed high, or shy with the rough riding boys" The Thomas who in "The force that through the green fuse drives the flower" had been gloomily aware that, at the same time, such procreative zest also "drives my green age" and "is my destroyer", now embraces his dearly-held vision of long-dead lovers, now dust in the grave. And the poem closes with the final triumphant assertion: "Hale dead and deathless do the women of the hill/ Love for ever meridian through the courters trees".

The women have made themselves immortal, and also those they loved and those they have borne. Their acts flash out to us from the darkness of the grave where they lie. As John Ackerman puts it in his *A Dylan Thomas Companion* (1991), " ... the poet celebrates their love as existing perpetually in nature".

After these tremendous assertions, 'Lament' is a somewhat unsatisfactory descent into what can only be described as bar-room comedy. It seems to me to be a poem written by a man for the consumption of 'the boys' between sups of ale. Even as a satire on Welsh chapel puritanism (if that is what is intended) it seems not to hit its targets with any particular or satisfying precision. An old man, now in decrepitude, mournfully considers a career of magnificent conquests: "When I was a windy boy and a bit/And the black spit of the chapel fold,/(Sighed the old ram rod, dying of women)".

Perhaps one simply shouldn't take it all too seriously. It reads like a notebook jotting that has found its way into the *Collected Poems* by mistake. Still, there is something disconcerting about a man facing his mortality as Thomas was, and being able to express that with such power, peddling this nonsense (which goes on for five repetitive stanzas) about a man's being 'worn out' by a life of sexual excess. It is public bar snigger. And if the point of the poem is meant to lie in the self-mocking realization that the mores of the chapel actually get the last laugh, the notion seems far outweighed by the smug satisfaction in the overheated recollection of past sexual exploits: "No springtailed tom in the red hot town/With every simmering woman his mouse ..." The 'roaring boy' is in charge here, boasting to his pub audience with a disparaging lewdness that sits oddly at this point in his œuvre, after the celebration of women he had given us in 'In the White Giant's Thigh'.

The much admired and anthologized 'Do not go gentle into that good night' is, by contrast, a manifestly deeply-felt performance, struggling as it does, to cope with the approaching death of the poet's father. It is cast as a villanelle (five tercets and a quatrain), which guarantees it formal limits that are not characteristic of Thomas's methods of composition. It has its moments, and the honesty of feeling behind it is never in doubt. But for such a short poem on such a serious subject it has too many moments of falseness to achieve that gem-like quality it so obviously strives towards. Perhaps, after all, the villanelle form shoe-horned Thomas into something that was not really his metier.

The first stanza achieves near perfection, but after that things almost immediately start going wrong. One cannot help feeling that Thomas, not being able to let his tried methods of composition have their head, is led into padding out thought simply to make the lines work. Why do "wise men at their end know dark is right"? It sounds bogus, something Thomas seldom is, even when he nears incomprehensibility. "Because their words had forked no lightning" sounds superficially to be working, but actually seems a shoddily pretentious way of saying that these men are aware that they have made no great waves in life.

In the next stanza, "The last wave by" seems not to have a satisfactory role except to make up the syllable count. The sense is that the last wave has already gone by. In which case, why bring it in here? What function does it serve? The metaphor, and the "crying how bright …" one which follows it (repeating the overriding idea of a sense of lives of failure), would only be effective if the wave were to be regarded as an impending doom which is yet to break over them. This does not seem to be the case. In any event the reader is caught in two minds. And that induced perplexity is fatal to the stanza's capacity to communicate with the clarity it so desperately needs, in a short lyric like this. It is not so much that we are overloaded with meaning – the common complaint against Thomas – but that we are always fishing for it here.

The final quatrain recaptures the perfect poise of sentiment with which the poem opened. But too much that happens in between has to be taken on trust. The manifest sincerity of the whole enterprise apart, a good deal of what David Holbrook has called "mimic wisdom" has had to be digested en route.

'Poem on his Birthday' restores us to the landscape of the Laugharne estuary, and Thomas to that confidence in his creativity which seems always to accompany the contemplation of it. It opens, apparently, in much the unvarnished descriptive mood that the earlier 'Poem in October' did.

But there is already a greater sense of direction. This day, five years on, is not, as its predecessor was, one of wide-eyed wonder, but will be spent "in the bent bay's grave". The poet himself both celebrates and spurns it. He is in no mood for childhood recollections. There is a strong feeling that, in between, something has, for better or worse, been accomplished, and that there is no going back on that. The poet sees himself, creatively spent, perhaps, washed up like flotsam on the shore he inhabits in "His driftwood thirty-fifth wind turned age". The elements of nature, which have become so familiar to us in these late poems, are themselves touched with an accompanying sombreness of mood. "Curlews aloud in the congered waves/Work at their ways to death". In 'Poem in October' gulls, rooks and larks had given him unfeignedly cheerful birthday greetings. Here, 'dying' and 'death' are the dominant themes.

The thirtieth birthday had been an occasion on which it was possible to look forward with the hope that creative vision and the will to express it might be kept intact when the poet revisited it 12 months hence. That does not seem to be important to the poet, now. Here, "tolls his birthday bell" recalls irresistibly to mind Donne's "Never send to know for whom the bell tolls".

Not that this is, for all the sombreness of tone, a gloomy poem. The poet is on terms of open-eyed acquaintanceship with whatever eternity it is that he stands on the brink of. He is going gladly "In the unknown, famous light of great/And fabulous, dear God." The repetitive liturgical refrain of the much earlier poem 'And death shall have no dominion' had lacked conviction. But, here, Thomas can utter the praises of "fabulous, dear God" without inviting the tiniest reflex of scepticism. It is a measure of the poetical journey he has made in between. The sun and the sea, the two most potent symbols in Thomas's poetical universe are with him. For Ann, he as the bard had called "all/The seas to service" in her praise. Now, for him, that same sea, with its leviathan population (the single word "tusked" suggests narwhals, walruses, marlins, elephant seals, imagine what you will) "exults" as it contemplates his progress.

The poem works up an irresistible momentum. By the final stanza the whole of nature seems to be riding alongside the poet, providing escort, as it were, to his stately farewell to this world, and passage to the next. Angels and their "mansouled fiery islands" are as effortlessly a part of Thomas's mental landscape as the familiar larks and "bouncing hills". The wonder is that he can bring them in together, here, without a flicker of dissent from the reader. There is an overwhelming sense in which, as far as the things of this world are concerned, for Thomas 'Ripeness is all'. Paradise is glimpsed, and the poet will take his leave of us on a surge of exaltation.

12

Under Milk Wood

It is difficult not to be drawn into a comparison of 'Poem on his Birthday' with Wordsworth's 'Intimations of Immortality'. Both poems are about memory and that tragic sense of the loss of wonder that accompanies growing up. Both are an attempt to embody for us their poets' perception of man's relationship, as he grows older, with the spiritual – as well as the human – universe.

Both, also and unmistakably, say farewell to the deepest springs of creativity. For Wordsworth: "The things that I have seen I now can see no more". While Thomas can now only: "cry with tumbledown tongue." A poet does not, perhaps, simply pack up (though Rimbaud did). Wordsworth was to soldier on for another forty years. But they were years in which he never again achieved the intensity of the *Lyrical Ballads,* the early books of *The Prelude,* or 'The Leech Gatherer'. Indeed, towards the end they give us the utter ghastliness of the 'Sonnets on the Punishment of Death'. By the end Wordsworth had become "Wordy Wordsworth" or "Wordsworst", as lesser men took to calling him.

Thomas, by contrast did give up – or, perhaps more accurately, simply stopped. 'Poem on his Birthday' was written in the summer of 1951. Long, barren years were not to stretch ahead of him, as they were with Wordsworth. But there were more than two years remaining (quite a long spell in terms of his short writing life) in which his creative energies were directed to something of a quite different kind.

There is no point criticizing *Under Milk Wood* for what it is not and does not set out to be. The moral sledgehammer that David Holbrook brought to it in his book *Llarreggub Revisited* landed many palpable hits, which reverberated for many years. Yet the object of chastisement was the wrong one in the first place for the points

Holbrook wanted to make about what he saw as the moral decline of modern literature.

Under Milk Wood has given great pleasure to generations: as a play for radio, the medium for which it was originally conceived; as a stage production; and as a film from Andrew Sinclair which successfully harnessed the talents of a small galaxy of stage and screen stars.

But is it literature, and did Dylan Thomas think it was? The answer to the first question, at any rate, surely has to be no, and the comparison with James Joyce's *Ulysses* which it invites (to some extent at Thomas's own suggestion), immediately indicates its short-comings on that level.

In *Ulysses* Joyce takes his protagonists – Stephen Dedalus and Leopold Bloom – on their respective journeys into the heart of darkness. He immerses them in the filth of the real world, with its male coarseness and insensitivity, female infidelity, secretions of both male and female bodily fluids, poverty, prostitution, lies and unkindnesses. After confronting them so unsparingly with their respective demons, he is able, without a shred of sentimentality, to restore them at the end to equanimity and a degree of faith. That faith is seen to be justified, after such a harrowing of hell, in the marvellous, naked outpourings of Molly Bloom which end *Ulysses* in a triumphant verdict of 'Yes', on her abused and cuckolded husband.

Under Milk Wood is superb entertainment of its kind, but it simply does not live in this sphere, nor for that matter in the rich oxygen of Thomas's finest poetry. The point is illustrated by *Under Milk Wood's* own Molly Bloom, Polly Garter. She is a promiscuously feckless coupler with men, whose sexual activities, apparently unregulated by any imperatives of birth control, burden her with a succession of infants. In life, such a woman could not help being, long before 30, especially in those days, maltreated and worn out by a succession of men with whom she must trade sex for money in order to survive. But this is not reality – a Polly Garter in a poor area in Cardiff – but Arcadia. And her response to her situation, as she croons to one of her babies is the cheerful: "Isn't life terrible – thank God!"

In the context of *Under Milk Wood* this actually gets a laugh not a groan. But it is a laugh that belongs in the music hall. In fact, as soon as we accept the play's music-hall credentials, it becomes not second rate, but first rate of its kind, humorous and with moments of genuine poignancy. (His acceptance of talent, rather than genius, as his presiding muse had not completely obliterated Thomas's finer perceptions, as his tender treatment of the Revd Eli Jenkins demonstrates.)

After the famous poetic prose scene-setting of *Under Milk Wood,* we are introduced to the first tranche of protagonists who inhabit the mythical village of Llarreggub. They are "Captain Cat, the retired blind seacaptain" and the long-dead shipmates who still haunt his dreams.

Landsman though he was, Thomas knows of the customs of the sea. The port of Swansea was a large and bustling one in his day. Though he did not choose to use either it, or the other elements of industrial or mercantile South Wales life, in his poetry, a sensibility so alive as his can hardly have failed not to be aware of them. Indeed his short stories indicate quite clearly that he was.

Here he perfectly catches both the essential simplicity of seagoing folk (including their predictable vices when let on shore), and the paternal relationship that exists between a good skipper and his men. There is something strangely moving in the childlike recital of such insignificant crimes as those related and disavowed. These men were drowned when huge seas swamped the decks of Captain Cat's command, S.S. *Kidwelly.* They will never make their home port to hear the answers to the questions they urgently put to him from the depths of Davy Jones's locker. To which Captain Cat, uneasily stirring in his bunk in that moment of truth before dawn, can only answer brokenly: "Oh, my dead dears!" It is a scene that never fails to be poignant, whether done just as a voice play or with a visual element as well.

There is also something very Welsh about it (pastiche Welsh, if you like). It certainly seems to demand Welsh accents as we read it, (though of course it was first performed by Americans, and we do not know at this distance what stab they made at the Cymric lilt). The distinguished cast of Andrew Sinclair's film – which included Richard Burton, Elizabeth Taylor, Peter O'Toole, Glynis Johns, Vivien Merchant, Sian Phillips, Rachel Thomas and Angharad Rees – certainly claimed it for Wales in their manner of speaking it.

The point is worth making that this 'Welshness' is completely absent from the poetry. Thomas studiedly erased his Welsh accent for reading purposes from an early age, and his recordings emphasize that his poetry is as surely a part of English literature as are the recordings from *Paradise Lost,* which he also rendered so magnificently for the BBC. But the difference between *Under Milk Wood* and the poetry is not just a matter of accent. The subject matter of the latter is universal, of the former, regional and local. As we have noticed, the moral life of the Arcadian Llarreggub is not translatable as far as Cardiff, much less to the East End of London.

As Larreggub's day begins to gather momentum, the Revd Eli Jenkins pads barefoot to his front door and delivers his daily verse homily to his beloved town. In a masterly piece of distancing Thomas turns a piece of local newspaper doggerel into something enchanting, even moving. Jenkins graciously concedes that Llarreggub Hill cannot be compared with the famed eminences of Snowdonia and the Cambrian Mountains. But it is when he turns his attention to the place of Milk Wood's brook in the scheme of other rivers that Thomas touches something near genius. We are expecting a modest dissent from comparison with Britain's most celebrated streams. Instead, Thomas gives us a catalogue of the largely unknown and unpronounceable. It is on one level totally absurd. And yet, by some miracle, it does not elicit the expected sneer from us.

In one point of view, like that memorable scene in Shakespeare's *King Henry IV* in which Shallow and Silence ruminate, in an out-of-the-way corner of Gloucestershire, on their place in the scheme of things, it is laughable in the extreme. And yet it touches on the pathos of a brave determination to persevere, even in the midst of the utter insignificance of human life. Like Silence, the Revd Eli Jenkins and his flock will be able to say no more, at the end, than that they "have been merry twice and once ere now". But it is enough to secure them a kind of immortality.

13

Dylan Thomas and his Critics

Thomas had died at the very pinnacle of his literary fame. The period between the reception of *Collected Poems 1934-1952* and the obituaries in newspapers and periodicals had been far too short for there to have been any revision of the estimate of his merits at that time. Semi-hysterical outpourings apart – and there were plenty of those – the sober judgement on him was that the world had lost a major literary figure. *The Times*, which had in its obituary of James Joyce a dozen years before completely failed to do the Irish author justice (and in doing so reaped the wrath of T.S. Eliot), was on this occasion determinedly in the van of praise for the Welshman.

Its obituary, prepared at short notice during Thomas's final coma, appeared on the day following his death. It pointed in his early poems to a "strong individuality in pattern-making and choice of language which was to distinguish him from all his fellow writers in maturity". It noted the advance to coherence in *The Map of Love*, in which "he has pared his imagery without losing any of its force", and concluded: "It is, however, upon the poems in *Deaths and Entrances* (1946) and in the few poems of the slim volume *In Country Sleep*, published in America in 1951, that his reputation as one of the greatest masters of English poetry is likely to rest."

Once the dust had settled – and there was a good deal of the obscuring non-literary sort such as Brinnin's *Dylan Thomas in America* and Caitlin's first essay, *Leftover Life to Kill* (both 1957) – a reaction to these large claims was inevitable. To the critics of the *Scrutiny* school, then riding high at Cambridge, with T.S. Eliot as their benchmark of what a modern poet should be, and F.R. Leavis as his formidable advocate, the work of Thomas was simply anathema. A popular fame such as he enjoyed was not, in any case, likely to appeal to *Scrutiny* elitism. And in so patently failing to conform to the dictum of Eliot that "The minimum requirement of good poetry is that it should have the virtues of good prose", Thomas put himself beyond the pale at the outset.

He was not helped by the 'Ern Malley' hoax in Australia. From 1944 onwards this ardent disciple of Thomas, had been publishing his dark and clotted work to great acclaim in the Adelaide periodical *Angry Penguins*. It was only later to be revealed that the entire output of this poet (who had, perforce, to die young) was the work of two highly inventive poet-editors who had knocked it together, by culling phrases randomly from a variety of sources, in a single day. Though at that stage Ern Malley's work had not found its way to London (his two creators blew the whistle on his career rather too early for maximum effect) the episode contributed to the impression among sceptics that 'anyone' could synthesize the hitherto much-admired verbal pyrotechnics of Thomas's verse.

The result was that Dylan Thomas studies, such as they have been (critical interest is still far outweighed by the biographical), got off to a start in a highly partisan atmosphere, with a good deal of mudslinging. People hate feeling gulled, and reaction to the chorus of acclaim was the more unforgiving for that. Robert Graves, with all the authority of a major poet, weighed in with the opinion that Thomas actually did not care what his poems meant, terms in which he was more or less seconded by the novelist and poet John Wain. Kingsley Amis made Thomas an extremely unsympathetic character, the poet Gareth Probert, in his novel *That Uncertain Feeling*, published in 1955. This was not, of course, a critical exercise as such. But in satirizing the accepted 'Welshness' of a man who knew no Welsh, Amis, always a master of the sneer, managed to plant the charge of bogusness, without having to stop to analyze it.

In this atmosphere such admirable moderation as that of G.S. Fraser's sympathetic but by no means uncritical essay *Dylan Thomas* of 1957 was liable to be drowned out in a torrent of sheer abuse. Battle was to be rejoined on the other side of the question by David Holbrook's terrific cannonade in *Llarreggub Revisited* of 1962. But it should be noted that the book has the subtitle *Dylan Thomas and the state of modern poetry*. Though it lands some shrewd blows on Thomas, it is just as unsparing about the poetry of such contemporaries as Amis. Holbrook was concerned about what he saw as the unrelenting cynicism of postwar English literature, and he was later to recant his view of Thomas in that respect, whatever other faults he continued to find in him.

In the meantime, Welsh critics, feeling themselves doubly duped, having previously so wholeheartedly embraced an emotionalism that is acknowledged as a national weakness, had also begun to turn against him. In 1955 a new champion and another Thomas – R.S. this time – had emerged with the publication of *Song at The Year's Turning* in that year. These poems, rooted in the hard-favoured soil of North Wales and describing the harsh life of the hill farmer, were the complete antithesis of Dylan's lushness. In his native country there was a tendency now to see in R.S. and not Dylan, the true Welsh virtues. In that the Welsh may well have been right. As a poet of community R.S. Thomas was certainly Welsh in a way Dylan was not and never pretended to be. And he was, much later in his life, to become even more so by learning the language and writing in it. But none of that had, nor has, anything to do with their relative merits as poets.

Among Welsh critics Aneirin Talfan Davies stayed true to Thomas, seeking to show in his book *Druid of the Broken Body* (1964) that Thomas was a Christian poet, and that the obscurities of many of his poems could be forgiven for their "remarkable insight into the sacramental nature of the universe". John Ackerman, too, has kept the faith. Since 1964, when his *Dylan Thomas: his life and work*, appeared, he also has viewed Thomas as a predominantly religious poet, and his analysis of the œuvre is presented, amplified, in *A Dylan Thomas Companion* (1991).

In general, critical activity had, in not much more than ten years after Thomas's death, greatly diminished his reputation (as opposed to his fame as a tourist artefact – that increased exponentially, and has never suffered a check). His weaknesses, easy to deride in the weaker, earlier poems, were pounced on and used to damn the whole. Even today, his admirers tend to take refuge in his 'religious' virtues, and in language of weak generalisation that actually does his strengths no great service.

In the literary histories there is, in general, a kind of health warning against his name. Thus the George Sampson *Concise Cambridge*

History of English Literature, whose chapters on the modern era have been so admirably revised by R.W. Churchill, lends greater weight to his "lack of imaginative organisation" and "emotional incoherence" than it does (somewhat lukewarmly) to "literary gifts which were never in doubt". There is a strong suggestion that his merits weigh no more heavily than those of Chatterton, of which Sampson had earlier observed that "the intrinsic value of his work is not great".

In *The New Pelican Guide to English Literature* C.B. Cox pays lip service to his "lyrical grandeur" but is, in the end, with those readers who "find Thomas's worship of life an evasion of the truth". In his masterly *Guide to Modern World Literature* Martin Seymour-Smith stigmatizes him as suffering "from an insensitivity to the meanings of words, a result of his inability to come to terms with reality". Seymour-Smith places him down in the company of Swinburne, Dowson and Francis Thompson.

These days, most of the writing that is done about him, by far, is biographical rather than critical, with the emphasis on the discovery of yet another letter, yet another mistress, yet more ways of enjoying a holiday in Swansea and Carmarthenshire with the 'Dylan trail' in mind. In such an atmosphere, with only a resolute, but not necessarily critically acute, band of enthusiasts shouting the odds for the poetry, it is inevitable that a dispassionate estimate is going to be hard to come by. Many critics, in particular, persist in the charge that Thomas was wilfully obscure, because it was a way for him of avoiding reality. I hope I have been able to show that a falling off the path of intelligibility is, rather, almost always a failure of control of the means of creation.

The aim of this study has been, without ignoring his faults, to demonstrate that Dylan Thomas's work has, indeed, great intrinsic value. His enduring qualities – those things he has to say to us – are of an altogether more substantial order in my opinion than those of a Chatterton in his century or of a Dowson in his. He is certainly head and shoulders above any other Welsh poet of the 20th century writing in English. His talent is far more than a minor one, and his finest poems will not suffer by being read in company with those of Yeats, Eliot or Hardy. When he is at his best (and let us remember for what long, long stretches such giants as Milton and Wordsworth are below theirs) Thomas is simply incomparable in his power to communicate – and inspire – a joyous faith in the worth of existence.

It is perhaps worth bringing in the verdict of Saunders Lewis, here. He was, in almost all ways, the antithesis of Thomas: Welsh nationalist, Welsh-language writer, a man who was prepared to go to jail (and did) in defence of his culture (a thing one can hardly imagine of Thomas). He was, in short, a man of very different kidney – in all save a shared conviction of the supreme value and overriding claim of poetry upon the attention of mankind. Yet he recognized of this noisier, sometimes attention-seeking competitor in the lists of letters that: "He sang of the glory of the universe when it was the fashion of every prominent poet in Europe to sing despairingly and with passion of the end of civilization."

Further Reading

Critical and biographical studies

Dylan Thomas by G.S. Fraser (1957). An early, essay-length study. While not glossing over its weaknesses, it concentrates on the poet's strengths, and is as good as any piece of criticism that has appeared since.

Dylan Thomas in America by John Malcolm Brinnin (1957). While Brinnin often demonstrates colossal naivety in this account covering this aspect of the last few years of Thomas's life, it is definitely worth reading for the insight it gives us into the self-doubt of the man and poet.

A Reader's Guide to Dylan Thomas by William York Tindall (1962). This series of guides produced some good studies of 'difficult' modern poets. Unfortunately this is not one of them, though it is helpful on some of the earlier poems.

Llareggub Revisited by David Holbrook (1962). This celebrated onslaught on Dylan Thomas and all his works (which Holbrook later recanted), though somewhat one-track in its perceptions, still makes immensely stimulating reading as a critique of modern poetry.

Dylan Thomas: His Life and Work by John Ackerman (1964, 1991). A straightforward, honest piece of work. Stronger perhaps on affection for its subject than on critical insight.

Druid of the Broken Body by Aneirin Talfan Davies (1964). The principal 'religious' interpretation of Thomas's works.

The Life of Dylan Thomas by Constantine FitzGibbon (1965). The first 'official' biography, but none the worse for that. FitzGibbon deeply understands the nature of creativity and the bohemian existence, and does not waste time moralising about either.

Dylan Thomas. New Critical Essays edited by Walford Davies (1972). Too many of these essays are in the sexually over-excitable category, as their titles: *Randy Dandy in the cave of Spleen*; *The Wanton Starer*, *Adder's Tongue on Maiden Hair*, etc. tend to betray.

My Friend Dylan Thomas by Daniel Jones (1977). As one of the countless 'friends' of Dylan Thomas who really can lay claim to the title, Jones is well qualified to give us such a memoir, which, disappointingly, becomes a ragbag of impressions that advance our understanding of the man and poet no further.

Dylan Thomas: The Biography by Paul Ferris (1977, 1999). Well-researched, knowledgeable and illuminating. Its acerbity makes an interesting contrast with FitzGibbon's account.

Double Drink Story : My Life with Dylan Thomas by Caitlin Thomas (1997). The third and most unsparing account of her life with the poet, it was published after her death. If it pulls no punches, its author is just as tough on herself. A no-holds-barred warning to women who want to be poets' muses.

Dylan Thomas: A New Life by Andrew Lycett (2003). A comprehensive account of the doings of the Thomas life, with more drinks, more women and more couplings making their appearance than ever before. But it is an account in which the poems, and the creative impulse behind them, are submerged under the domestic detail.

GREENWICH EXCHANGE BOOKS

STUDENT GUIDES

Greenwich Exchange Student Guides are critical studies of major or contemporary serious writers in English and selected European languages. The series is for the student, the teacher and 'common readers' and is an ideal resource for libraries. The *Times Educational Supplement* praised these books, saying, "The style of these guides has a pressure of meaning behind it. Students should learn from that ... If art is about selection, perception and taste, then this is it."

(ISBN prefix 1-871551- applies)

All books are paperbacks unless otherwise stated

The series includes:

W.H. Auden by Stephen Wade (36-6)
Honoré de Balzac by Wendy Mercer (48-X)
William Blake by Peter Davies (27-7)
The Brontës by Peter Davies (24-2)
Robert Browning by John Lucas (59-5)
Samuel Taylor Coleridge by Andrew Keanie (64-1)
Joseph Conrad by Martin Seymour-Smith (18-8)
William Cowper by Michael Thorn (25-0)
Charles Dickens by Robert Giddings (26-9)
Emily Dickinson by Marnie Pomeroy (68-4)
John Donne by Sean Haldane (23-4)
Ford Madox Ford by Anthony Fowles (63-3)
The Stagecraft of Brian Friel by David Grant (74-9)
Robert Frost by Warren Hope (70-6)
Thomas Hardy by Sean Haldane (33-1)
Seamus Heaney by Warren Hope (37-4)
Gerard Manley Hopkins by Sean Sheehan (77-3)
James Joyce by Michael Murphy (73-0)
Philip Larkin by Warren Hope (35-8)
Poets of the First World War by John Greening (79-X)
Laughter in the Dark – The Plays of Joe Orton by Arthur Burke (56-0)
Philip Roth by Paul McDonald (72-2)
Shakespeare's *Macbeth* by Matt Simpson (69-2)
Shakespeare's *Othello* by Matt Simpson (71-4)
Shakespeare's *The Tempest* by Matt Simpson (75-7)
Shakespeare's Non-Dramatic Poetry by Martin Seymour-Smith (22-6)
Shakespeare's Sonnets by Martin Seymour-Smith (38-2)

Shakespeare's *The Winter's Tale* by John Lucas (80-3)
Tobias Smollett by Robert Giddings (21-8)
Dylan Thomas by Peter Davies (78-1)
Alfred, Lord Tennyson by Michael Thorn (20-X)
William Wordsworth by Andrew Keanie (57-9)

OTHER GREENWICH EXCHANGE BOOKS

LITERATURE & BIOGRAPHY

Matthew Arnold and 'Thyrsis' *by Patrick Carill Connolly*
Matthew Arnold (1822-1888) was a leading poet, intellect and aesthete of
the Victorian epoch. He is now best known for his strictures as a literary
and cultural critic, and educationist. After a long period of neglect, his
views have come in for a re-evaluation. Arnold's poetry remains less well
known, yet his poems and his understanding of poetry, which defied the
conventions of his time, were central to his achievement.
The author traces Arnold's intellectual and poetic development, showing
how his poetry gathers its meanings from a lifetime's study of European
literature and philosophy. Connolly's unique exegesis of 'Thyrsis' draws
upon a wide-ranging analysis of the pastoral and its associated myths in
both classical and native cultures. This study shows lucidly and in detail
how Arnold encouraged the intense reflection of the mind on the subject
placed before it, believing in " ... the all importance of the choice of the
subject, the necessity of accurate observation; and subordinate character
of expression."
Patrick Carill Connolly gained his English degree at Reading University
and taught English literature abroad for a number of years before returning
to Britain. He is now a civil servant living in London.
2004 • 180 pages • ISBN 1-871551-01-61-7

The Author, the Book and the Reader *by Robert Giddings*
This collection of essays analyses the effects of changing technology and
the attendant commercial pressures on literary styles and subject matter.
Authors covered include Charles Dickens, Tobias George Smollett, Mark
Twain, Dr Johnson and John le Carré.
1991 • 220 pages • illustrated • ISBN 1-871551-01-3

Aleister Crowley and the Cult of Pan *by Paul Newman*
Few more nightmarish figures stalk English literature than Aleister Crowley
(1875-1947), poet, magician, mountaineer and agent provocateur. In this
groundbreaking study, Paul Newman dives into the occult mire of Crowley's

works and fishes out gems and grotesqueries that are by turns ethereal, sublime, pornographic and horrifying. Like Oscar Wilde before him, Crowley stood in "symbolic relationship to his age" and to contemporaries like Rupert Brooke, G.K. Chesterton and the Portuguese modernist, Fernando Pessoa. An influential exponent of the cult of the Great God Pan, his essentially 'pagan' outlook was shared by major European writers as well as English novelists like E.M. Forster, D.H. Lawrence and Arthur Machen.

Paul Newman lives in Cornwall. Editor of the literary magazine *Abraxas*, he has written over ten books.

2004 • 223 pages • ISBN 1-871551-66-8

John Dryden *by Anthony Fowles*

Of all the poets of the Augustan age, John Dryden was the most worldly. Anthony Fowles traces Dryden's evolution from 'wordsmith' to major poet. This critical study shows a poet of vigour and technical panache whose art was forged in the heat and battle of a turbulent polemical and pamphleteering age. Although Dryden's status as a literary critic has long been established, Fowles draws attention to Dryden's neglected achievements as a translator of poetry. He deals also with the less well-known aspects of Dryden's work – his plays and occasional pieces.

Born in London and educated at the Universities of Oxford and Southern California, Anthony Fowles began his career in film-making before becoming an author of film and television scripts and more than twenty books. Readers will welcome the many contemporary references to novels and film with which Fowles illuminates the life and work of this decisively influential English poetic voice.

2003 • 292 pages • ISBN 1-871551-58-7

The Good That We Do *by John Lucas*

John Lucas's book blends fiction, biography and social history in order to tell the story of his grandfather, Horace Kelly. Headteacher of a succession of elementary schools in impoverished areas of London, 'Hod' Kelly was also a keen cricketer, a devotee of the music hall, and included among his friends the great Trade Union leader Ernest Bevin. In telling the story of his life, Lucas has provided a fascinating range of insights into the lives of ordinary Londoners from the First World War until the outbreak of the Second World War. Threaded throughout is an account of such people's hunger for education, and of the different ways government, church and educational officialdom ministered to that hunger. *The Good That We Do* is both a study of one man and of a period when England changed, drastically and forever.

John Lucas is Professor Emeritus of the Universities of Loughborough and Nottingham Trent. He is the author of numerous works of a critical and scholarly nature and has published seven collections of poetry.

2001 • 214 pages • ISBN 1-871551-54-4

In Pursuit of Lewis Carroll *by Raphael Shaberman*
Sherlock Holmes and the author uncover new evidence in their investigations into the mysterious life and writing of Lewis Carroll. They examine published works by Carroll that have been overlooked by previous commentators. A newly discovered poem, almost certainly by Carroll, is published here.

Amongst many aspects of Carroll's highly complex personality, this book explores his relationship with his parents, numerous child friends, and the formidable Mrs Liddell, mother of the immortal Alice. Raphael Shaberman was a founder member of the Lewis Carroll Society and a teacher of autistic children.

1994 • 118 pages • illustrated • ISBN 1-871551-13-7

Liar! Liar!: Jack Kerouac – Novelist *by R.J. Ellis*
The fullest study of Jack Kerouac's fiction to date. It is the first book to devote an individual chapter to every one of his novels. *On the Road, Visions of Cody* and *The Subterraneans* are reread in-depth, in a new and exciting way. *Visions of Gerard* and *Doctor Sax* are also strikingly reinterpreted, as are other daringly innovative writings, like 'The Railroad Earth' and his "try at a spontaneous *Finnegans Wake*" – *Old Angel Midnight*. Neglected writings, such as *Tristessa* and *Big Sur*, are also analysed, alongside better-known novels such as *Dharma Bums* and *Desolation Angels*.

R.J. Ellis is Senior Lecturer in English at Nottingham Trent University.

1999 • 295 pages • ISBN 1-871551-53-6

Musical Offering *by Yolanthe Leigh*
In a series of vivid sketches, anecdotes and reflections, Yolanthe Leigh tells the story of her growing up in the Poland of the 1930s and the Second World War. These are poignant episodes of a child's first encounters with both the enchantments and the cruelties of the world; and from a later time, stark memories of the brutality of the Nazi invasion, and the hardships of student life in Warsaw under the Occupation. But most of all this is a record of inward development; passages of remarkable intensity and simplicity describe the girl's response to religion, to music, and to her discovery of philosophy.

Yolanthe Leigh was formerly a Lecturer in Philosophy at Reading University.
2000 • 57 pages • ISBN: 1-871551-46-3

Norman Cameron *by Warren Hope*
Norman Cameron's poetry was admired by W.H. Auden, celebrated by Dylan Thomas and valued by Robert Graves. He was described by Martin Seymour-Smith as, "one of ... the most rewarding and pure poets of his generation ..." and is at last given a full length biography. This eminently sociable man, who had periods of darkness and despair, wrote little poetry by comparison with others of his time, but it is always of a consistently high quality – imaginative and profound.
2000 • 221 pages • illustrated • ISBN 1-871551-05-6

POETRY

Adam's Thoughts in Winter *by Warren Hope*
Warren Hope's poems have appeared from time to time in a number of literary periodicals, pamphlets and anthologies on both sides of the Atlantic. They appeal to lovers of poetry everywhere. His poems are brief, clear, frequently lyrical, characterised by wit, but often distinguished by tenderness. The poems gathered in this first book-length collection counter the brutalising ethos of contemporary life, speaking of and for the virtues of modesty, honesty and gentleness in an individual, memorable way.
2000 • 47 pages • ISBN 1-871551-40-4

Baudelaire: Les Fleurs du Mal *Translated by F.W. Leakey*
Selected poems from *Les Fleurs du Mal* are translated with parallel French texts and are designed to be read with pleasure by readers who have no French as well as those who are practised in the French language.
F.W. Leakey was Professor of French in the University of London. As a scholar, critic and teacher he specialised in the work of Baudelaire for 50 years and published a number of books on the poet.
2001 • 153 pages • ISBN 1-871551-10-2

'The Last Blackbird' and other poems by Ralph Hodgson *edited and introduced by John Harding*
Ralph Hodgson (1871-1962) was a poet and illustrator whose most influential and enduring work appeared to great acclaim just prior to and during the First World War. His work is imbued with a spiritual passion for the beauty of creation and the mystery of existence. This new selection

brings together, for the first time in 40 years, some of the most beautiful and powerful 'hymns to life' in the English language.

John Harding lives in London. He is a freelance writer and teacher and is Ralph Hodgson's biographer.

2004 • 70 pages • ISBN 1-871551-81-1

Lines from the Stone Age *by Sean Haldane*

Reviewing Sean Haldane's 1992 volume *Desire in Belfast*, Robert Nye wrote in *The Times* that "Haldane can be sure of his place among the English poets." This place is not yet a conspicuous one, mainly because his early volumes appeared in Canada, and because he has earned his living by other means than literature. Despite this, his poems have always had their circle of readers. The 60 previously unpublished poems of *Lines from the Stone Age* – "lines of longing, terror, pride, lust and pain" – may widen this circle.

2000 • 53 pages • ISBN 1-871551-39-0

Shakespeare's Sonnets *by Martin Seymour-Smith*

Martin Seymour-Smith's outstanding achievement lies in the field of literary biography and criticism. In 1963 he produced his comprehensive edition, in the old spelling, of *Shakespeare's Sonnets* (here revised and corrected by himself and Peter Davies in 1998). With its landmark introduction and its brilliant critical commentary on each sonnet, it was praised by William Empson and John Dover Wilson. Stephen Spender said of him "I greatly admire Martin Seymour-Smith for the independence of his views and the great interest of his mind"; and both Robert Graves and Anthony Burgess described him as the leading critic of his time. His exegesis of the *Sonnets* remains unsurpassed.

2001 • 194 pages • ISBN 1-871551-38-2

The Rain and the Glass *by Robert Nye*

When Robert Nye's first poems were published, G.S. Fraser declared in the *Times Literary Supplement*: "Here is a proper poet, though it is hard to see how the larger literary public (greedy for flattery of their own concerns) could be brought to recognize that. But other proper poets – how many of them are left? – will recognize one of themselves."

Since then Nye has become known to a large public for his novels, especially *Falstaff* (1976), winner of the Hawthornden Prize and The Guardian Fiction Prize, and *The Late Mr Shakespeare* (1998). But his true vocation has always been poetry, and it is as a poet that he is best known to his fellow poets. "Nye is the inheritor of a poetic tradition that runs from Donne and Ralegh to Edward Thomas and Robert Graves," wrote James Aitchison in 1990, while the critic Gabriel Josipovici has described him as "one of the most interesting poets writing today, with a voice unlike that of any of his contemporaries".

This book contains all the poems Nye has written since his *Collected Poems* of 1995, together with his own selection from that volume. An introduction, telling the story of his poetic beginnings, affirms Nye's unfashionable belief in inspiration, as well as defining that quality of unforced truth which distinguishes the best of his work: "I have spent my life trying to write poems, but the poems gathered here came mostly when I was not."

2005 • 133 pages • ISBN 1-871551-41-2

Wilderness *by Martin Seymour-Smith*

This is Martin Seymour-Smith's first publication of his poetry for more than twenty years. This collection of 36 poems is a fearless account of an inner life of love, frustration, guilt, laughter and the celebration of others. He is best known to the general public as the author of the controversial and bestselling *Hardy* (1994).

1994 • 52 pages • ISBN 1-871551-08-0

BUSINESS

English Language Skills *by Vera Hughes*

If you want to be sure, (as a student, or in your business or personal life), that your written English is correct, this book is for you. Vera Hughes's aim is to help you to remember the basic rules of spelling, grammar and punctuation. 'Noun', 'verb', 'subject', 'object' and 'adjective' are the only technical terms used. The book teaches the clear, accurate English required by the business and office world. It coaches acceptable current usage and makes the rules easier to remember.

Vera Hughes was a civil servant and is a trainer and author of training manuals.

2002 • 142 pages • ISBN 1-871551-60-9